30 Days With God In Tight Places

Seeking God In The Psalms
When We Find Ourselves Between A Rock And A Hard Place

I0533355

Maurice Smith

Publisher
Rising River Media
risingrivermedia.org

Cover Design
Cover design by Gale A. Smith
Composition & Layout by Lawton Printing, Spokane
Stock Photo licensed from Freepik.com

ISBN 13
979-8-218-48283-1

Table of Contents

An Introduction To Tight Places

A Personal Journey

The new year was starting out busy. As a documentary filmmaker on homelessness, the beginning of the new year found me filming a documentary at the City Church Warming Shelter in Spokane.* In spite of the COVID-19 pandemic, the previous year had been surprisingly productive. I had released my second documentary, "The Hidden Homeless: Families Experiencing Homelessness." As the year progressed, I filmed and released my third documentary, "Give Me Shelter: The Story of the Cannon Street Warming Center," and began filming my fourth documentary, "The Least of These: Communities of Faith Serving the Homeless."

I was working to finish filming "The Least of These" when I took a break for my annual physical, required by my health insurance. I felt good. Everything was normal, as far as I knew, when my doctor said, "We've never done a PSA test on you. Let's do one so we have a baseline to work from." The PSA, or Prostate-Specific Antigen test, is standard screening protocol for prostate cancer. When my blood panels came back, my doc said everything looked normal (except my tri-gylcerides, which have always run high), but my PSA was slightly elevated. What should have been a "4" was a "6.5" ("10" is considered the warning threshold). "I'm not worried about it," he told me, "but I'm going to send you to a urologist and have him take a look." Little did I know that my personal *tight place* was beginning.

Six weeks after my annual exam I sat in the office of an excellent Urologist who, thankfully, knew exactly what to do. Two weeks later I found myself in an MRI machine. The report came back. Positive for prostate cancer. Small and contained, but still cancer. My *tight place* was tightening. A targeted biopsy a month later confirmed the MRI. I had prostate cancer. It not only confirmed my cancer, it placed me firmly *between a rock and a hard place*. More tests were needed. There were treatment options to be discussed, advanced directives to be completed, and consents to be signed. Three months after the biopsy I had a radical prostatectomy, the most common surgery for prostate cancer in generally healthy men of my age, when the cancer hasn't spread beyond the prostate. Such cancer frequently spreads to become bone cancer, something much more difficult (and painful) to treat. Thankfully, my cancer had not spread. Following surgery, a series of ultra-sensitive PSA tests confirmed that I was cancer free.

My *tight place* slowly loosened its grip on my life (and the life of my wife and family). I came to realize how very thankful we all were for God's deliverance in

> Sometimes what God is doing through our tight places only becomes clear in hindsight.

response to our prayers and to the prayers of many others. Only three years later did it dawn on me that my experience could become the opening story about those life moments the Psalmist refers to as *tight places*. Sometimes what God is doing through our *tight places* only becomes clear in hindsight.

A Life-Long Journey of Faith

The tight places of life come to us in a wide variety of disguises. They come disguised as financial challenges, relationship struggles (especially among family members), health issues, conflicts with business partners, employers, or co-workers, legal battles, and misunderstandings that turn friends into "enemies." Any list of potential conflicts and tight places would be longer than anything we could include here. Use your own life-experiences, and your imagination, and you'll quickly figure out the tight places that God has allowed and used in your own life.

As believers on a life-long journey of faith, we often find ourselves challenged - even overwhelmed - by pressures, people, and situations that cause us to cry out to God for His intervention and help. The authors of the Psalms understood. Under the inspiration of the Holy Spirit, they poetically described their own life challenges as *tight places*, writing and singing about them as part of their personal and

> And who among us doesn't want or need God to be "exceedingly present" in the tight places of our life.

corporate worship. Some four dozen Psalms (roughly one-third of all the Psalms) reflect the struggles of the Psalmists in the midst of life's tight places (you'll find a complete list of these Psalms in "Appendix - All The Psalms of Tight Places" at the end of this devotional).

One of those Psalms - the one that actually started my journey of understanding the work of God in our *tight places* - is Psalm 46. In the opening verse, the Psalmist, Korah, declares, "God is our refuge and strength, a very present help in trouble." While that is good English, it misses the more literal sense of the Hebrew, "*God to us, a refuge and strength, an exceedingly present help in tight places.*" And who among us doesn't want or need God to be "exceedingly present" in the tight places of our life. I did. And I'm fairly certain you do, too.

While the intervening centuries may separate us from the Psalmist, our experiences and our struggles connect us. We've all experienced the struggle of tight places on our collective journey of faith through this world and into the Kingdom of God. In the Kingdom

> In the Kingdom of God, the tight places of life are the fertile soil of our spiritual growth.

of God, the tight places of life are the fertile soil of our spiritual growth. Our challenge is to drive our spiritual roots deep into the soil of our tight places, allowing them to both teach us and test us. Our tight places test our soul, because an untested soul is an immature soul. In the Kingdom of God, spiritual maturity is the product of spiritual truth experienced over time, often in the tight places of life. I'm pretty sure the Psalmists would agree.

Between a Rock and a Hard Place

We discover the biblical concept of tight places in the Hebrew root word *tsarar*. It broadly refers to something tight, narrow, or confining; a place so narrow we can only travel in one direction.* As a verb, it means *to bind, to be or make narrow*, or *to be in or to cause distress*. The root word and its various forms appear seventy-eight times in the Psalms describing people or circumstances that create a *tight place* in our life. The Psalmists frequently use *tsarar* to describe *enemies, foes,* or *adversaries* - people who force us into *tight places* and cause us anguish and distress. You and I might describe all of this simply as finding ourselves pressed "between a rock and a hard place." In the hands of the biblical writers, the idea of tight places becomes a metaphor for a host of different struggles the people of God have faced over the centuries in our shared spiritual journey into the Kingdom of God.

> You and I might describe all of this simply as finding ourselves pressed "between a rock and a hard place."

Times Change, People Don't

Biblical Hebrew can be both beautifully poetic and very down-to-earth. We see this on full display in the Psalms. No where is this better illustrated than in the poetic description of life's challenges as *tight places*, as the biblical writers express their deep personal anguish and cry out to God for help, deliverance, and comfort.

You and I might think our present day struggles are very different from those of people who lived thirty centuries ago. But the reality is, while times may have changed, people have not. They struggled with friends who betrayed them, and so do we. They experienced struggles with dysfunctional family members, and so do we. They experienced being misunderstood, even persecuted, for their faith and obedience, and so do we. And they found themselves in circumstances that they thought would crush them and that challenged their faith to the breaking point. And so do we.

Years pass and times change, but people and their struggles remain much the same, as does our God Who remains the same yesterday, today, and forever, and Who remains an exceedingly present help in our *tight places*.

Life Through the Lens of the Kingdom

"Jesus answered him, "Truly, truly, I say to you, unless one is born again he cannot see the kingdom of God." (John 3:3)

Everyone who has believed in Jesus, the Christ, for their salvation has been born again. And everyone who has been born again can now "see" and has now "entered" the Kingdom of God (John 3:5). Jesus preached the Kingdom, taught the Kingdom, and modeled the Kingdom. The early church continued Jesus' proclamation of the Kingdom. The author of

> The Kingdom of God is the lens that brings all of God's dealings with us into focus, including our tight places.

the book of Acts (Luke) concludes his account of the early church by describing the ministry of Paul in Rome with these words, "He lived there two whole years at his own expense, and welcomed all who came to him, proclaiming the Kingdom of God and teaching about the Lord Jesus Christ with all boldness and without hindrance" (Acts 28:30-31).

Why is this important in our study of *tight places?* Because the Kingdom of God is the lens that brings all of God's dealings with us into focus, including our tight places. Everything God does in and through us and our tight places gives evidence of His Kingdom at work in the lives of His people here and now, while preparing us (and perhaps those around us)for our future life in that Kingdom which is yet to come.

Like seed sown in a field, the Kingdom of God grows organically and unpredictably, "The kingdom of God is as if a man should scatter seed on the ground. He sleeps and rises night and day, and the seed sprouts and grows; *he knows not how"* (Mark 4:26-27). How often have you and I declared, in the midst of our tight place, "I don't know what God is doing!"? Welcome to organic life and learning in the Kingdom, where God sows and sprouts seeds of faith and obedience in us, while sowing the seed of a challenged faith in the lives of those around us who are touched by what God is doing in our lives. Like the ripple effects of a stone dropped into still water, the "Kingdom ripple effects" of

> In the Kingdom of God, the lessons of our tight places spread organically, like seed sown for a growing harvest.

God's dealings with us in our tight places spread out to touch, challenge, and encourage an ever-widening circle of lives, prodding them to reflect on and respond to what God is doing. In the Kingdom of God, the lessons of our tight places spread organically, like seed sown for a growing harvest.

Discover Your Ebenezer

The word *Ebenezer* is a compound Hebrew word that literally means "stone of the help." It comes from an event (yes, a tight place) recorded in 1 Samuel 7:1-12. There, at a place called Mizpah, the prophet Samuel erected a memorial - an Ebenezer - to mark the place, just north of Jerusalem, where God helped Israel defeat the Philistines, "Then Samuel took a stone and set it up between Mizpah and Shen and called its name Ebenezer; for he said, 'Till now the LORD has helped us'" (1 Samuel 7:12).

In our journey through the Psalms of tight places, an Ebenezer is an insight, a principle, or a life lesson that reminds us of what God has done for us. We record them so we don't forget. In every tight place you and I experience, an Ebenezer stone is waiting for us to discover, to reflect, and to remember all that God has done and is doing for us during our season of tight places. Our spiritual growth in the Kingdom depends on our willingness to allow His truth to change us as we experience it over time, often in the tight places of our journey. Ebenezers can take a variety of forms. A promise from Scripture that we claim because it spoke to us. An new insight offered about our shared spiritual journey in the Kingdom of God. An unexpected devotional thought from the Psalms of tight places. At the end of each devotional you'll have an opportunity to reflect and write about what you've discovered, and to identify an Ebenezer you feel God is calling you to remember as you move forward on your journey into His Kingdom.

> In every tight place you and I experience, an Ebenezer stone is waiting for us to discover, to reflect, and to remember all that God has done and is doing for us during our season of tight places.

How To Get The Most From Your "30 Days"

May I Suggest A Good Bible Version? I would encourage you to read each Psalm in a good version of the Bible before reading the study. It isn't a requirement, but it would help. The scripture quotes in these devotionals are from the English Standard Version (ESV) Study Bible, one of the best Study Bibles of the past thirty years or more. I would encourage you to secure one. You'll find the ESV notes on each Psalm very helpful. *

Depth Versus Breadth. In his excellent commentary on the Gospel of John, Leon Morris reminds his readers that John's Gospel has been described as "a pool in which a child may wade and an elephant can swim."* The same could be said about the Psalms of tight places. Think of it as the difference between breadth and depth. While there is something in it for every believer who has ears to hear, this devotional study is intended for depth. In the Kingdom of God,

> In the Kingdom of God, discipleship is about depth, not breadth.

discipleship is about depth, not breadth. This devotional study is intended to challenge you to reflect more deeply on your walk with God and your discipleship with Jesus and His Kingdom.

Repetition. As in most other areas of life, repetition is an important key to our discipleship. It takes time and repetition to fully embrace and eventually embody spiritual truths. We learn by repetition until the repeated lesson becomes second nature. As you reflect on these devotional studies, ask yourself what themes are being repeated and why they are important.

Tested and Challenged. The Psalmists tell us that God is a refiner of metal Who tests the hearts and challenges the character of His people (More about this in "Day 26, Psalm 81" when we look at Psalm 66:10). What area of your life is God testing and challenging through each devotional?

Connecting the Old With the New. "For whatever was written in former days was written for our instruction, that through endurance and through the encouragement of the Scriptures we might have hope" (Romans 15:4). The New Testament completes what the Old Testament begins. Take the time to ask yourself what connects the lesson of the Psalmist with similar lessons taught and developed more fully in the New Testament. Such connections teach and remind us that Scripture is made of "whole cloth" rather than being a "patchwork quilt."

Follow the Asterisk. Whenever an asterisk (*) appears, there is a corresponding note at the end of the book under "Notes on the Psalms" organized by the Day and the Psalm. It's impossible to thoroughly treat every Hebrew term that our study will uncover. So, the "Notes" will define important terms and point the interested reader to a reference source where they can find more information.

Pace Yourself. This devotional study in the Psalms of tight places will challenge you to pace yourself. The goal isn't to read quickly and move on. The goal is to read well, and to reflect. And that takes time. This isn't your 3-minute devotional. And while these devotional studies are laid out as a series of 30-day devotionals, you may find yourself lingering longer over them. And that's okay. So whether daily, every other day, or once a week, take the time to allow each devotional to have its impact. God isn't in a hurry. He knows that refining the metal of human character takes time. He will wait for you, if you're willing to wait on Him.

Sermons and Lessons. If you are a pastor or a small group leader, think of these "30 Days" (actually, 31) as seeds for sermons, and lessons and discussion topics for your small group. People in your circle of friends, your fellowship, your congregation, or your small group are

> Most people suffer silently, rather than publicly.

struggling in tight places that you may be completely unaware of. Most people suffer silently, rather than publicly. Their lives and their discipleship in the Kingdom are being impacted and challenged as they deal with the fear and chaos of their personal tight place. They quietly wonder if they're alone in their struggle, if their experience is strange for God's people, if God has forgotten them or is hiding His face from them, and what a biblical response to their tight place might be. They need the encouragement and hope that the Scriptures and the Holy Spirit can give them. My prayer is that you - and they - will find that encouragement and that hope in the devotions that follow.

Remember. Finally, as you turn the page and begin your journey through the tight places of the Psalms, take a moment to remember and reflect on God's faithfulness in your own life. A journey through the tight places of the Psalms is a journey through God's faithfulness to His struggling people, including you and me. To say it more personally, it is through the tight places of our life that we discover God's faithfulness. Without the tight places He allows into our life, we could never discover the fortress of His

> A journey through the tight places of the Psalms is a journey through God's faithfulness to His struggling people, including you and me.

protection, the kindness of his mercy and compassion, the depth of His steadfast covenant-keeping love, and His faithfulness to both deliver us and never give up on us in our weakest and darkest moments. In the words of the Apostle Paul to his young protégée, Timothy (who had his own tight places yet to face):

> "The saying is trustworthy, for:
> If we have died with him, we will also live with him;
> if we endure, we will also reign with him;
> if we deny him, he also will deny us;
> if we are faithless, he remains faithful -
> for he cannot deny himself."
> (2Timothy 2:11-13)

Reflections On "An Introduction To Tight Places"
Take few minutes to reflect on what you've discovered through today's devotional.

Insights You Discovered To Reflect On

✍

✍

✍

Raising Your Ebenezer
An Ebenezer is an insight, a principle, or a life lesson that reminds us of what God has done - or is doing - for us on our journey through our tight places. What Ebenezer did you discover for yourself in today's devotional? Use this space to write it out here:

Notes

My Thoughts, Insights, And Reflections

_____
_____
_____
_____
_____
_____
_____
_____
_____
_____

Day 1
The Tightest Place Of All

"... that we, being delivered from the hand of our enemies,
might serve him without fear,
in holiness and righteousness before him all our days."
(Luke 1:74-75)

A Morning Like Any Other

The day began like any other day. Up early. My son was off to high school, a precocious sophomore. My wife had a routine dental appointment for a filling. My daughter and I decided to conduct our morning home schooling activities (reading world history and practicing some math problems) down at our favorite coffee shop where I could sip a gourmet brew with a chocolate chip cookie and she could nurse a hot chocolate, complete with a fine head of whipped cream.

My daughter and I were mid-way through our coffee and chocolate when the store owner (a personal friend) told me I had a phone call.

"Hello?" I answered. "Mr. Smith?" came the reply, "This is the nurse at the dentist's office. Sir, your wife has had an adverse reaction to the anesthetic, and we would like for you to come to the office."

Too stunned to ask any questions I agreed and hung up the phone. When my daughter and I arrived at the office my heart sank to find a waiting ambulance in the parking lot. Holding back my questions and emotions, I raced up to the third floor dental office (yes, with my daughter in-tow). There I discovered paramedics hovering over the semi-conscious form of my wife, Gale. They were preparing to take her to the emergency room of the local hospital.

By God's grace, this story had a happy ending. At the hospital the attending physician concluded that the problem was only an overdose of epinephrine (synthetic adrenalin) which, combined with the anesthetic, had been injected directly into a blood vessel, causing an "adrenalin rush" and dizziness. Gale soon recovered and was back at the dentist's office later that day for her routine filling.

Later, as I reflected on the events of the day, the Lord reminded me of Psalm 46:1-3, "God is our refuge and strength, a very present help in trouble. Therefore we will not fear, though the earth should change, and though the mountains slip into the heart of the sea; though its waters roar and foam, though the mountains quake at its swelling pride." That morning I had felt two things. First, I had felt my personal earth suddenly shake. Second, I had felt genuine raw fear.

A Tight Place Called Fear

Fear is an ancient tight place with deep spiritual roots. It has plagued the human race ever since that moment in the Garden of Eden when fear gripped Adam and Eve over their sin and caused them to hide from God's Presence. Fear has kept us hiding from God ever since.

As I noted earlier, and will repeat over the course of these devotionals, *tight places* come in many different forms. But they all have one thing in common - their unique ability to strike fear into the human heart. Without question, raw fear is by far one of the most common and powerful human emotions. Fear embodies our most visceral responses to life's unforseen or unavoidable events, "enemies" that come to us in a wide variety or forms and disguises. Fear of an injured loved one, fear of financial failure and loss, fear of a failing or broken relationship and our inability to fix it, fear of failing health and its many personal consequences, fear of people who threaten or attempt to hurt us, fear of our spiritual journey being misunderstood by those around us, fear that we've misunderstood what we thought were God's promises or directions toward us, fear that our prayers will go unanswered (or that the answer will be "no"), fear that our faith has been in vain (or isn't up to the challenge we're facing), fear that God's Word can't be trusted to address our practical problems. And the list goes on. Feel free to add your unique fears to the ever growing list of fears that haunt the human heart, even among believers.

A Common Theme. Fear is a common theme among God's people. Just how common? Let's take a look. The primary word for fear in the Old Testament (*yare* - "to fear or be afraid") occurs 334 times in 324 verses, embracing a wide variety of people and circumstances. Forty-seven of those

> In the Kingdom of God, confronting our fears is an important part of biblical worship.

occurrences are in the Psalms - ancient Israel's worship song-book. In the Kingdom of God, confronting our fears is an important part of biblical worship. The Hebrew phrase "Do not fear" or "fear not" occurs seventy-six different times. Forty-five of those involve God telling His people to "fear not," while thirty-one times involve people encouraging each other to "fear not." In the New Testament, the primary Greek words for "fear" (*phobos*, "fear" and *phobeo*, "to be afraid") occur some 140 times, including thirty-three times where God, Jesus, or angelic messengers, tell specific people, "Don't be afraid."

But perhaps the strongest evidence for fear as one of the tightest places (if not *the* tightest) in the experience of God's people is found in Luke Chapter 1. There, Luke recounts how the angel Gabriel confronted Zachariah, the soon-to-be father of John the Baptizer. When Zachariah expressed unbelief at the idea that two old people could bear a son, Gabriel struck him unable to speak until God's promise was fulfilled. When the day of John the Baptizer's dedication arrived, Zachariah regained his voice.

In what is now known as the *Benedictus* (Luke 1:67-80), Zachariah praised God for the coming Messiah whose ministry John would announce and prepare the way for. According to Zachariah, the coming Messiah would make it possible "that we, being delivered from the hand of our enemies, might serve him without fear, in holiness and righteousness before him all our days" (Luke 1:74-75). One of the blessings the coming Messiah would secure on behalf of His people would be "deliverance from the hand of our enemies" and the ability to "serve Him without fear." How strong is the spiritual tight place of fear? So strong that it requires the redemptive work of Jesus on the cross to break its grip on our hearts.

Vertical and Horizontal Fear. In the Kingdom of God, dealing with our fears is both a vertical and a horizontal exercise. The horizontal exercise is about how we respond to our "enemies," those people and circumstances that cause fear and force us into a tight place. The vertical exercise is about how we respond to God in faith and obedience as He works in us, shaping our spiritual ability to "serve Him without fear."

A.W. Tozer once observed, "Water cannot rise above its own level. Neither can a Christian by any sudden spasmodic effort rise above the level of his own spiritual life."* We teach and impart to others who we are, what we know, and what we've experienced and learned. You and I cannot disciple others and impart meaningful spiritual truth if we refuse to allow God to teach us those spiritual truths through His word and through the shaping and refining process we experience in the tight places of our life. It's how God raises the water level of our spiritual lives. In the Kingdom of God, the tight places of our journey are the potter's wheel where God fashions Christ-likeness from the clay of our life, including our ability to "serve Him without fear."

> In the Kingdom of God, the tight places of our journey are the potter's wheel where God fashions Christ-likeness from the clay of our life.

God has a purpose for every tight place He allows into our life, part of His process of discipleship in the Kingdom of God. Every tight place we encounter is a discipleship lesson, a new step forward in our personal growth and maturity, an opportunity to grow as we embrace fresh truths about God and about our life in His Kingdom. God also wants to use every tight place you and I experience to inspire hope in others. Believers who have confronted their own tight place of fear are in a much better place to encourage struggling fellow believers to confront their own tight place of fear. We are able to comfort others because we have been comforted by God (2 Corinthians 1:4). Only then are we equipped to teach others to do the same. It was true of Job and his tight place, it was true of

David and his many tight places, and it's true of you and me and our tight places, starting with the greatest tight place of all: fear.

From Fear And Chaos to Cosmos And Shalom

Fear and *chaos* tend to walk hand in hand through the tight places of our life. *Chaos* and fear are tell-tale signs that the "Enemy of our soul" is at work. But the eye of faith also sees God at work, bringing us through fire and flood and into a broad place of *cosmos* and *Shalom* (Psalm 66:12).

In the Kingdom of God, *cosmos* is the order He creates out of the *chaos* of our brokenness, including the brokenness of our fears. The God we worship and serve is the same God who turned the *chaos* of a formless void and darkness into the *cosmos* and order of creation (Genesis 1). And as Gideon discovered when fear gripped his own heart, we worship a God Whose name is *Jehovah-Shalom*, "The LORD Is Peace"(see Judges 6:23-24). In the midst of the tight places of our life, God moves to turn the *chaos* of our tight places into the *cosmos* of His Kingdom order, and to give us the peace and wholeness of His *Shalom*.*

> In the Kingdom of God, *cosmos* is the order He creates out of the *chaos* of our brokenness, including the brokenness of our fears.

What tight place is striking fear into your heart today? Whatever it is, God is allowing it, challenging you to confront and overcome both your circumstances and your fears. He wants to demonstrate His power to turn the *chaos* and fear of your tight place into the *cosmos* and *Shalom* of His Kingdom purposes for your life. He wants to teach you to be fearless, fearing nothing but Him alone. And the first step is to place the *chaos* and fear of your tight place at His feet as an act of personal repentance and worship, "Then Gideon built an altar there to the LORD and called it, 'The LORD Is Peace'" (Judges 6:24). When you and I can find genuine *Shalom* in the midst of tight places that would otherwise fill us with fear, that's when we discover what it means to take refuge, to find shelter, and to abide in the Shadow of the Almighty.

O Lord, our God, with a spoken word You turned a universe of chaos into the cosmos and order of Your creation. Do the same for us today. Lord, we bring the chaos and fear of our tight place to You and lay them at Your feet as an act of faith, of personal repentance, and worship. Speak and turn the chaos and fear of our tight place into the cosmos and Shalom of Your Kingdom purposes. This we ask in the Name of Jesus, our redeemer and Prince of Shalom. Amen.

Reflections On "Day 1 - The Tightest Place of All"

Take few minutes to reflect on what you've discovered through today's devotional

Insights You Discovered To Reflect On

✎

✎

✎

Raising Your Ebenezer

An Ebenezer is an insight, a principle, or a life lesson that reminds us of what God has done - or is doing - for us on our journey through our tight places. What Ebenezer did you discover for yourself in today's devotional? Use this space to write it out here:

Notes

My Thoughts, Insights, And Reflections

_____

_____

_____

_____

_____

_____

_____

_____

30 Days With God In Tight Places

Day 2
Psalm 3
Overwhelmed By A Thousand Troubles

"O LORD, how many are my foes!
Many are rising against me;
many are saying of my soul,
'There is no salvation for him in God'."
(Psalm 3:1-2)

Honestly, there are times in our lives when we feel absolutely overwhelmed by life's problems. The pressures of life mount to the point where we feel like we're being crushed and forced into a *tight place* with no apparent solution or way out. If that's true of you today, then you and David have something in common. We read about David's *tight place* in 2 Samuel (chapters 15 through 19), where he eventually found himself in deep trouble and overwhelmed. A palace coup was quietly underway, led by David's own son, Absalom. And that deserves a quick story.

Absalom was David's son by his third wife, Maacha, the daughter of the King of Geshur (see 1 Chronicles 3:2). Growing up, Absalom was the kind of young man who stood out in a crowd. "Now in all Israel there was no one so much to be praised for his handsome appearance as Absalom," says the author of 2 Samuel. "From the sole of his foot to the crown of his head there was no blemish in him" (2 Samuel 14:25). Physically, Absalom was "a looker." But he was also a problem child with a tumultuous relationship with his father, King David. The King loved his wayward son, but Absalom didn't return that love. When another of David's sons, Amnon, sexually assaulted David's daughter, Tamar, Absalom spent two years biding his time and plotting his revenge, and Amnon's murder. There were more incidents (see 2 Samuel 13-14) which revealed Absalom's true character - unforgiving, daring, reckless, foolhardy, ambitious, and covetous with his eye set on David's throne. A storm was brewing.

That brewing storm of *troubles* reached a breaking point in 2 Samuel 15 when Absalom mounted a palace coup. It was serious, so serious that David was forced to flee his own capital in order to avoid capture and even death. People David had previously trusted turned against him, betraying him, and taunting him that not even God could save him, "many are saying of my soul, 'There is no salvation for him in God'" (3:1-2).

And that's where Psalm 3 picks up the story. In today's Psalm, an overwhelmed David records the spiritual struggle he experienced during his time of fleeing for his life, exclaiming in the opening verse, "O Lord, how many are my foes!" An important Hebrew root (*rabab*) forms the heartbeat of this passage.* In verses one and two, that root is translated *many*, and in verse six it's translated *many thousands* (or *ten thousand* in the KJV). Together, these verses communicate a growing sense of overwhelming numbers and overwhelming problems.

In the opening verse of the Psalm, the word *foes* is our now-familiar Hebrew root word for *tight places*. Foes, enemies, and adversaries are people whose behavior forces us into situations best described as *tight places*. David felt overwhelmed by a myriad of problems created by a myriad of people who were pushing him into a tight place with no visible way out. For their part, they honestly thought they had succeeded so well that they could openly boast that not even God could save him, "There is no salvation for him in God" (3:2). But that's not where the story ends.

> Foes, enemies, and adversaries are people whose behavior forces us into situations best described as *tight places*.

Psalm 3 easily divides into three parts. In Part one (vs 1-2), David describes how overwhelmed, surrounded, and boxed in he felt by people who were forcing him into a very tight place. But in Part 2 (vs 3-6), David pulls back the curtain on his relationship with God, "But you, O LORD, are a shield about me, my glory, and the lifter of my head."

David understood that the God of Israel was his shield and protection. David knew that when he "cried aloud" to God in prayer, God would answer and sustain him. Living in the light of that reality, David chose not to be afraid of "many thousands of people" who were causing him problems and forcing him into an impossibly tight place. Finally, in Part 3 (vs 7-8), David acknowledges God's protection against his enemies, declaring, "Salvation belongs to the Lord." Yes, it does, both for David and for us.

So, did David really have ten thousand people problems? Probably not, but it felt like it. And sometimes our lives feel that way, too. A few very real problems become "many thousands" in our mind as the Enemy of our soul taunts us and wages spiritual warfare against us, whispering in our ear, "there is no salvation for you in God." We simply become emotionally and spiritually overwhelmed. But from David's experience of finding himself forced into an impossibly tight situation, by a son he loved and by people he had trusted, we can learn how to face our own *tight places*. Like David, we can remember that God is our shield and defender against any and all pressures brought against us. Knowing that God is our shield and defender, we can cry out in faith and with confidence that God will hear us and answer us in our moment of need. And, like David, in the midst of life's overwhelming pressures, we can lie down and sleep in peace (*Shalom*), because the God Whose name is *Jehovah-Shalom* ("the

Day 2 - Overwhelmed By A Thousand Troubles

Lord is Peace") will sustain us. Even when we feel surrounded and overwhelmed by "many thousands" of people or problems, we can choose faith over fear and boldly declare, "Salvation belongs to the Lord." Yes, it does, both for David and for us.

O Lord, our God, today we cry out with David who declared, "O Lord, how many are my foes!" Like David, we feel overwhelmed by what looks like a myriad of problems created by a myriad of people pushing us into a tight place with no visible way out. But You, O LORD, are a shield about us, our glory, and the lifter of our head. You are Jehovah-Shalom and we pray for Your peace. Empower us by Your Spirit to choose faith over fear, to lie down and rest in peace, and to boldly declare, Salvation belongs to the Lord! For Jesus' sake and in His Name we ask it. Amen

Reflections On "Day 2 - Psalm 3 - Overwhelmed By A Thousand Troubles"
Take few minutes to reflect on what you've discovered through today's devotional

Insights You Discovered To Reflect On

✍

✍

✍

Raising Your Ebenezer
An Ebenezer is an insight, a principle, or a life lesson that reminds us of what God has done - or is doing - for us on our journey through our tight places. What Ebenezer did you discover for yourself in today's devotional? Use this space to write it out here:

Notes

My Thoughts, Insights, And Reflections

_____

_____

_____

_____

_____

_____

_____

_____

_____

Day 3
Psalm 4
Quietly Trusting

"Answer me when I call, O God of my righteousness!
You have given me relief when I was in distress.
Be gracious to me and hear my prayer!"
(Psalm 4:1)

Our Psalm today opens with David letting us know that he has been - and perhaps still is - in a *tight place*, a place of *distress*. David never tells us anything specific about his distress (a little more about this later). But it doesn't really matter. After all, we seldom discover life lessons by focusing on our problems. We discover the truths of the Kingdom - and lessons for our own life - when we focus on God, on His dealings with us, and on our responses.

Making Room. David begins by offering a prayer acknowledging God's deliverance, "You have given me relief when I was in distress" (Psalm 4:1). The word "relief" (*rachab*) literally means "to make room," and "distress" is our familiar Hebrew word for a *tight place.** A more literal translation might be, *You have made room for me in my tight places.* And that's where

> God often answers our prayers by meeting us in our tight places and making room for us.

we discover our first life lesson: God often answers our prayers by meeting us in our tight places and *making room* for us. He gives us some short-term relief that eases some of the immediate pressure. He isn't done with us yet, but He gives us *breathing room.* The resolution of our tight place comes later.

Praying Boldly. God's answer to David's prayer motivates David to boldly pray and ask God to "Be gracious to me and hear my prayer." There's an extra life lesson here that we could easily miss: Answered prayer should motivate us to pray even more. We see this

> Don't stop praying just because God has answered!

lesson lived out in the life of Moses in Exodus 33:13 where he prays, "Now therefore, if I have found favor in your sight, please show me now your ways, that I may know you in order to find favor in your sight." Having found favor in answer to his prayers, Moses prays for more favor. Lesson: Don't stop praying just because God has answered!

Tribulation In Tight Places. The *tight places* of the Psalms offer us a metaphor for the life pressures all believers experience as "sojourners and exiles" (1 Peter 2:11) in a world system that is not our ultimate home. Jesus warned His disciples that they would experience such life pressures in this world. The Old Testament calls these life pressures *tight places*. The New Testament calls them *tribulation*. How do we know the two are related in a common experience among God's people? When the Hebrew Old Testament was translated into Greek (the

> The tight places of the Old Testament become the tribulations of the New Testament.

Septuagint), the Hebrew words for *tight places* were most commonly translated with the Greek word *thlipsis* (tribulation, affliction).* We find that Greek word in John 16:33 where Jesus tells His disciples, "I have said these things to you, that in me you may have peace. In the world (*cosmos*)* you will have tribulation. But take heart; I have overcome the world." The *tight places* of the Old Testament become the *tribulations* of the New Testament.

A Clash Of Values. Jesus would soon tell Governor Pilate that His Kingdom was not of this world order. This present world system is filled with pressures - *tribulations*. As disciples of the Kingdom, our values - those of the Kingdom - ultimately clash with the values of this present world system. We shouldn't be surprised to find ourselves under pressure or in tight places, as the conflicting values of these two different worlds collide. We serve a

> As disciples of the Kingdom, our values - those of the Kingdom - ultimately clash with the values of this present world system.

different King, and we serve a different Kingdom. And that reality inevitably produces conflicts and *tight places*. David experienced them. Jesus promised them. The early church encountered them. Tight places. Tribulation. The pressures of life. These are the common experience of God's people, causing us - like David - to cry out, "Be gracious to me and hear my prayer."

Attacking What Is Honorable. David offers a few hints about the distress of his own tight place when he says, "O men, how long shall my honor be turned into shame? How long will you love vain words and seek after lies?" (4:2) Apparently, unnamed people attacked David's honor, attempting to turn what was honorable in David's life into something shameful. Some people are so attached to this present world system, and so opposed to the Kingdom of God, that they are willing to "love vain words and seek after lies." When the values of the Kingdom conflict with the values of this present world system, people often respond by attacking us and those values in a vain attempt to turn something honorable (like faith, obedience, compassion, fidelity, sexual purity, and more) into something shameful.

A People Set Apart. Responding to these attacks, David offers us another life lesson. In the midst of his *tight place*, David found comfort in his relationship with God, "But know that the LORD has set apart the godly for himself; the LORD hears when I call to him." (4:3) David understood what it meant to be set apart by God for Himself. Do we?

Set Apart In The Old Testament. The idea of God setting His people apart for Himself - literally, making a distinction between those who are His and those who are not - is found in both the Old and New Testaments. In the Old Testament, the word "set apart" (*pala*)

> David understood what it meant to be set apart by God for Himself. Do we?

appears seven times.* It carries the sense of making or marking a distinction between two things. We find it in Exodus 8:22 where God "set apart the land of Goshen," making a distinction between God's people (who lived in Goshen) and the rest of Egypt. We see it again in Exodus 9:4 during the fifth plague when God made "a distinction between the livestock of Israel and the livestock of Egypt," preventing the livestock of Israel from dying. Later, in Exodus 33:16, Moses makes a case before God that His presence among the people of Israel would distinguish them "from every other people on the face of the earth."

Set Apart In The New Testament. This theme of separation or distinction for God's people carries forward in the New Testament with the Greek word *aphorizo* ("to mark off with boundaries," or "to separate"). We find it in Matthew 25:32 where Jesus describes a coming day of judgment when the Son of Man "will separate (*aphorizo*) people one from another as a shepherd separates the sheep from the goats." We also find it in Acts 13:2 where the Holy Spirit speaks to the early Church, setting people apart for ministry, "Set apart for me Barnabas and Saul for the work to which I have called them."

But perhaps the strongest connection between the Old and New Testament ideas of God distinguishing His people from all others and setting them apart for Himself is found in 2 Corinthians 6:17-18, "Therefore go out from their midst, and be separate from them, says the Lord, and touch no unclean thing; then I will welcome you, and I will be a father to you, and you shall be sons and daughters to me, says

> How do your lifestyle and your responses to your tight places set you apart from those around you?

the Lord Almighty." Here the Apostle Paul draws on God's command to Israel in Isaiah 52:11 and applies it to the Church, declaring that the Church is the fulfillment of God's covenant people who are now being restored under the new covenant. Both David in Psalm 4 and Paul in 2 Corinthians want their readers to understand that God separates and distinguishes His people from all others.

He sets us apart. How do your lifestyle and your responses to your tight places set you apart from those around you by demonstrating the values of the Kingdom of God?

A Four-Fold Response. Out of his experience in this tight place, David offers us another lesson about how believers should respond to such times. A well-worn truism reminds us, "We can't control what happens (or what people do), but we can control how we respond." Under the inspiration of the Holy Spirit, David offers us his own four-fold response to his tight place.

Anger without sin. Anger is the all-too-human response to a wide assortment of life situations where we feel abused, lied to, lied about, treated unfairly, misunderstood, or generally disrespected (or see others being treated that way). "Be angry, and do not sin" (4:4a) is David's counsel. But is it possible to be angry and not sin? Yes. According to the Apostle Paul in Ephesians 4:26, "Be angry and do not sin; do not let the sun go down on your anger." In the Greek text, Paul's words in Ephesians 4 are a direct quotation from the Greek translation of the Old Testament. Paul is quoting David, but adding, "do not let the sun go down on your anger." How does anger not become sin? By dealing with it quickly (before the sun goes down), confessing our anger to the Lord, and by yielding our tight place, including those who caused it, over to Him to resolve, rather than foolishly acting on our anger.

Quiet reflection. Rather than acting on our anger and engaging in foolish words or actions in our tight place, David counsels quiet reflection, "ponder in your own hearts on your beds, and be silent" (4:4b). Quiet, honest reflection often becomes honest and effective prayer.

Obedience. The Old Testament system of sacrifices ended with the sacrifice of Jesus for sin to satisfy all the requirements of the Law. The only remaining sacrifices are our individual sacrifices of obedience, praise, and thanksgiving. In the midst of our tight places, our calling as believers is to praise and thank God that He is still in control, and to obey His will and purposes as best we understand them.

Trust. This is where we discover David's fourth and most important response of all - trust. We never truly know the depth of anyone's faith (including our own) until we witness the depth of his or her trust in the midst of life's tight places. The anger we experience in our tight place must give way to quiet reflection, effective prayer, genuine obedience, and absolute trust that God is bigger than any tight place we find ourselves

> We never truly know the depth of anyone's faith (including our own) until we witness the depth of his or her trust in the midst of life's tight places.

in. He is able to "make room for us."

Finally, David appreciates the struggles of believers who are crying out to God in their own personal distress, "There are many who say, 'Who will show us some good?' Lift up the light of your face upon us, O LORD!" (4:6) David offers his experience as proof that, through anger without sin, quiet reflection, effective prayer, genuine obedience, and absolute trust, every believer can find joy, peace, and safety in the tight places of life, "You have put more joy in my heart than they have when their grain and wine abound. In peace I will both lie down and sleep; for you alone, O LORD, make me dwell in safety" (4:7-8).

O Lord, our God, we give You thanks this day for being the God of our tight places. Thank You for making room for us in our distress and tribulations, for setting us apart for yourself and your Kingdom purposes, and for giving us the grace we need to resolve our anger without falling into sin. Father, teach us the power of quiet reflection, of effective prayer, of sacrificial obedience, and of absolute trust. In the midst of our tight places, empower us to declare with David, "In peace I will both lie down and sleep; for you alone, O LORD, make me dwell in safety." In Jesus Name we ask it, Amen.

Reflections On "Day 3 - Psalm 4 - Quietly Trusting"
Take few minutes to reflect on what you've discovered through today's devotional

Insights You Discovered To Reflect On

✎

✎

✎

Raising Your Ebenezer
An Ebenezer is an insight, a principle, or a life lesson that reminds us of what God has done - or is doing - for us on our journey through our tight places. What Ebenezer did you discover for yourself in today's devotional? Use this space to write it out here:

Notes

My Thoughts, Insights, And Reflections

_____

_____

_____

_____

_____

_____

_____

_____

Day 4
Psalm 6
Mercy And Grace

"Be gracious to me, O LORD, for I am languishing;
heal me, O LORD, for my bones are troubled.
(Psalm 6:2)

A *Troubled Soul.* Our Psalm opens with a troubled soul and the words of someone who barely has the strength to pray. It's a cry for mercy and grace against divine discipline that the Psalmist knows he deserves, "rebuke me not in your anger, nor discipline me in your wrath." This is the cry of a guilty but repentant heart. A cry so deep that the Psalmist (David) is troubled right down to his bones (again, welcome to Hebrew metaphor). David is hurting from his bones to his soul, "my bones are troubled . . . . My soul also is greatly troubled"(6:3-4). How "troubled" is David's soul? The word "greatly" (*me'od*) carries a sense of "vehemently."* David's soul is vehemently, almost violently, troubled, with a hurt so deep that he feels like he's going to die. How do we know? Because David asks God to spare his life, reminding Him that "in death there's no remembrance of you; in Sheol who will give you praise?" (6:5) I think we can safely say that David was in a *tight place.*

A *Cry For Mercy.* Like so many of us, David needed the kind of spiritual healing that only God can provide. He needed the healing that comes from God's gracious (but undeserved) intervention, "Be gracious to me, O LORD, for I am languishing; heal me, O LORD, for my bones are troubled" (6:2). The word "gracious" (*chanan*) appears seventy-seven times in the Old Testament, including thirty-two times in the Psalms.* The KJV consistently translates it "mercy." The ESV translates it "gracious." Both are right. It's the heartfelt, kind, and merciful response of someone who has something to give, toward someone who has a need. God in His mercy is kind toward those who have a need, but who don't deserve His help. And let's face it. None of us do. David understood this truth, so he pairs his cry for God's mercy with an appeal to His steadfast love, "save me for the sake of your steadfast love" (6:4). Whether it springs from God's mercy or from His steadfast love, David needs God's intervention and healing. He needs God's deliverance from the consequences of his own behavior.

> God in His mercy is kind toward those who have a need, but don't deserve His help.

Consequences. Like David, you and I often experience the consequences of choices or behaviors we later regret. In that very common and human experience, we are no different from David, and David is no different from us.

Centuries may separate us, but our poor choices, behaviors, and consequences unite us in a heartfelt cry to God for His mercy and grace.

Mercy And Grace In Action. Like complementary bookends, the New Testament often completes what the Old Testament begins. The mercy and grace David longed for finds its ultimate fulfillment in the New Testament book of Hebrews, where the author encourages his readers with these words, "Let us then with confidence draw near to the *throne of grace,* that we may *receive mercy* and *find grace* to help in time of need" (Hebrews 4:16). Mercy is God's love in action, relieving our suffering and delivering us from the well deserved consequences of our choices and behaviors. God's grace is His undeserved favor in action, bestowing blessings we don't deserve and could never earn. And, like David, we need both mercy and grace.

> Mercy is God's love in action, relieving our suffering and delivering us from the well deserved consequences of our choices and behaviors.

Exhaustion. David's words in this Psalm reveal a deep personal reality. David is exhausted. Our struggle with the tight places of life can leave us physically, emotionally and spiritually exhausted. We can almost feel the emotional exhaustion in David's voice, "I am weary with my moaning; every night I flood my bed with tears; I drench my couch with my weeping. My eye wastes away because of grief; it grows weak because of all my foes" (6:6-7).

Foes And Tight Places. The word *foes* at the end of verse seven is our Hebrew root for *tight places.* It encompasses all the people, and the problems they caused, that forced David into this tight place. And *foes* is a good description of both the very tangible human conflict and the unseen spiritual conflict. In the New Testament, the Apostle Paul reminds us that, ". . . we do not wrestle against flesh and blood, but against the rulers, against the authorities, against the cosmic powers over this present darkness, against the spiritual forces of evil in the heavenly places" (Ephesians 6:12). All too often we forget that the foes we can see are only part of a larger struggle that's underway as the Kingdom of God and the domain of darkness do battle in our *tight place* (Colossians 1:13). And the intensity of that conflict often leaves us exhausted.

Confident Praying. There is no question that David felt exhausted as a result of his struggle in this tight place. But David didn't allow his exhaustion to overshadow his faith. He might be weary, but he still believed in God's ultimate answer, and in his own ultimate victory. And so he concludes with a confident declaration that God has heard his prayers and will respond, "Depart from me, all you workers of evil, for the LORD has heard the sound of my weeping. The

Day 4 - Mercy And Grace

LORD has heard my plea; the LORD accepts my prayer" (6:8-9). By faith, David embraced the spiritual reality that, while his victory over his tight place was yet to come, God had heard and answered his prayers.

Today's Psalm reminds us that, as believers, sometimes we pray and believe through tears and exhaustion in the midst of life's tight places. David understands. In another Psalm, he reminds his readers that God "[keeps] count of my tossings; put my tears in your bottle. Are they not in your book?" (Psalm 56:8). In the Kingdom of God no tears and no prayers - especially those in our tight places - are ever wasted or passed over uncounted . . . or unanswered.

> In the Kingdom of God, no tears and no prayers are ever wasted or passed over uncounted . . . or unanswered.

O Lord, our God, we worship You this day, exhausted and needy in the midst of our tight place as we deal with the consequences of our own choices and behaviors. Deliver us in Your mercy, and in Your grace grant us blessings we do not deserve. By faith we embrace the truth that none of our tears or prayers are ever wasted or passed over, and that our ultimate victory over our tight place is assured for the sake of your great Name, and the matchless Name of Jesus. Amen.

Reflections On "Day 4 - Psalm 6 - Mercy And Grace"
Take few minutes to reflect on what you've discovered through today's devotional

Insights You Discovered To Reflect On

✍

✍

✍

Raising Your Ebenezer
An Ebenezer is an insight, a principle, or a life lesson that reminds us of what God has done - or is doing - for us on our journey through our tight places. What Ebenezer did you discover for yourself in today's devotional? Use this space to write it out here:

Notes

My Thoughts, Insights, And Reflections

_____

_____

_____

_____

_____

_____

_____

_____

Day 5
Psalm 7
Accusations And Innocence - Part 1

"O LORD my God, in you do I take refuge;
save me from all my pursuers and deliver me."
(Psalm 7:1)

Our Psalm opens with a mystery, "A *Shiggaion of David, which he sang to the LORD concerning the words of Cush, a Benjaminite.*" Who is Cush? This Psalm is a song that David sang to God about "the words of Cush." So, who is Cush, and how could his "words" motivate David to write this Psalm?

Who Is Cush (And Why Is It Important)? What little we know about Cush is by association. He came from the tribe of Benjamin, which was also the tribe of King Saul. Saul spent much of his kingly reign trying to capture or kill David because he regarded David as a rival to his throne. After all, early in Saul's reign the prophet Samuel - at God's instruction - had anointed David as the future King of Israel, "And the LORD said, 'Arise, anoint him, for this is he.' Then Samuel took the horn of oil and anointed him in the midst of his brothers. And the Spirit of the LORD rushed upon David from that day forward" (1 Samuel 16:12-13). From that point on, Saul had an anointed, and more gifted, rival.

Anger And Hatred. We can only imagine how King Saul's anger and hatred toward David sowed the seed of anger and resentment within the tribe of Benjamin. Years later, when King David fled Jerusalem during the rebellion of his son, Absalom, a man named Shimei, a member of the tribe of Benjamin and "the family of the house of Saul," cursed David as he fled, "And Shimei said as he cursed, 'Get out, get out, you man of blood, you worthless man! The LORD has avenged on you all the blood of the house of Saul, in whose place you have reigned, and the LORD has given the kingdom into the hand of your son Absalom. See, your evil is on you, for you are a man of blood'" (2 Samuel 16:7-8).

Shimei's curse revealed an intense degree of unresolved anger - even hatred- festering in the tribe of Benjamin toward David. Then, in the wake of Absalom's rebellion and death, another Benjaminite named Sheba led much of the tribe of Benjamin in a rebellion against King David (see 2 Samuel 20:1ff). It just never seemed to end. And then, along came someone named Cush, another Benjaminite, whose words motivated David to write this Psalm.

Refuge. "O LORD my God, in you do I take refuge; save me from all my pursuers and deliver me, lest like a lion they tear my soul apart, rending it in pieces, with none to deliver" (7:1b-2). The word "take refuge" (*chasah*) shows up twenty-five times in the Psalms.* While it means "to take refuge," it carries the sense of *to trust in* (especially in the KJV). We take refuge in God because we trust Him. Like David, we trust God and place ourselves in His hands because that's where we find our peace - our *Shalom* - regardless of the outcome. Any peace that depends on the outcome isn't the *Shalom* of genuine faith.   Reading David's words in light of his struggles with the tribe of Benjamin, we get a sense that this isn't about Saul or persecution. Saul

> Any peace that depends on the outcome isn't the Shalom of genuine faith.

was gone and had been for several years. David and Israel had moved on. But someone from the tribe of Benjamin hadn't moved on and still harbored deep anger and hatred toward David. He still wanted to tear David's soul apart, "rending it in pieces." Some people simply don't know how to forgive or to move on. This was a personal attack against David's character. The "words of Cush" were about slander, involving false accusations of bribes, treachery, and betrayal, "O LORD my God, if I have done this, if there is wrong in my hands, if I have repaid my friend with evil or plundered my enemy without cause, let the enemy pursue my soul and overtake it, and let him trample my life to the ground and lay my glory in the dust. Selah" (7:3-5).

There Are Enemies, And Then There Are Enemies. The first Hebrew word translated *enemy* in verse 4 is our root word for *tight places.* An enemy is someone who forces us into a *tight place.* But in verse 5, David uses a second, more generic, word for enemy (*'ayab*) that communicates an underlying sense of "hostility" or "hatred" toward others.* Using these two words together, David expresses this person's intent. This "enemy" is someone motivated by hostility, even hatred, toward David. It's no accident or coincidence that this person is forcing David into a tight place. That was their intent from the outset.

At the beginning of this Psalm, we asked the question, "Who is Cush?" Perhaps we now have a better answer. We can't know for certain, but it seems that Cush was acting on accumulated grievances from the tribe of Benjamin, left over from the days of conflict between David and Saul, or more recently from the rebellion of Sheba. His actions were motivated by the lingering effects of past conflicts and hurts which were still fresh in his mind and drove him to make false and slanderous accusations in an attempt to impugn David's character. For Cush, it was time to settle old scores.

A Plea of Innocence. David's response offers an interesting plea before God. He maintains his innocence. To paraphrase David's response here, *"If I am guilty, let my enemy pursue, overtake, and trample me."* David's plea is interesting because, as David himself knew all too well, none of us is truly innocent. An anonymous Psalmist declares elsewhere, "If you, O LORD, should mark iniquities, O Lord, who could stand?" (Psalm 130:3). The clear implied answer is "no one." And David himself was keenly aware of his own sinfulness, declaring in Psalm 51, "For I know my transgressions, and my sin is ever before me. Against you, you only, have I sinned and done what is evil in your sight, so that you may be justified in your words and blameless in your judgment" (Psalm 51:3-4). Those are the words of someone who understands their own sinfulness. David isn't pleading his sinlessness, but his innocence in this particular matter. He's innocent of the false accusations being made against him. I think you and I can draw at least two lessons from this episode.

> "If you, O LORD, should mark iniquities, O Lord, who could stand? But with you there is forgiveness, that you may be feared."
> (Psalm 130:3-4)

First, we live in a world of guilt by accusation. To be publicly accused is to be presumed guilty in the court of public opinion. Is that wrong? Yes, it is, but it isn't new. David experienced it, too. The day may come when you or I are falsely accused of things we did not do, and sins we did not commit. Maybe old issues from our past, that we dealt with long ago, are revisited by people who were uninvolved but still take offense. We know both the truth and our innocence, but we're "guilty by accusation" in the eyes of others. As in David's situation, those false accusations may come from someone with genuine hostility and anger toward us for reasons that are not clear, but they are very intentional in their desire to force us into a tight place. Only you and God know the truth when you are falsely accused. If you have dealt with the issue before God, learn to stand on that truth. He is our refuge. Trust Him.

Second, avoid carrying around and spreading past grievances, especially the grievances of people and situations you weren't personally involved with (in the New Testament, that's the sin of gossip). Holding on to anger - and its first cousin, bitterness - is like drinking poison and expecting the other person to die. It doesn't work that way. Carrying around uninformed and unresolved grievances and anger keeps the fire

> Holding on to anger - and its first cousin, bitterness - is like drinking poison and expecting the other person to die.

of conflict burning, but you are the one who gets burned the worst. The writer of Proverbs wisely reminds us, "For lack of wood the fire goes out, and where there is no whisperer, quarreling ceases. As charcoal to hot embers and wood to fire, so is a quarrelsome man for kindling strife" (Proverbs 26:20-21). By carrying around some perceived grievance from a past conflict, you may be the one preventing resolution and healing, while kindling on-going strife. Eventually, you may cause someone to be "guilty by accusation" and force them into a tight place of your unjust creation. The soul destroyed by this poison won't be theirs. It will be yours.

There's more. In the Kingdom of God, there always is. And we'll explore that "more" in tomorrow's devotional.

O Lord our God, we worship You today as our God who seeks us, finds us, meets us in the tight places of our life. You are our refuge, the One we trust in the midst of the storm. Today we give You thanks that, in a world of falsehoods and "guilt by accusation," we can find refuge, truth and Shalom in Your Presence. Father, today we ask You to empower us to be Shalom-makers who practice forgiveness and reconciliation, and who choose not to keep the fires of conflict burning. In Jesus' Name and for His sake we ask it. Amen.

Reflections On "Day 5 - Psalm 7 - Accusations And Innocence - Part 1"

Take few minutes to reflect on what you've discovered through today's devotional

Insights You Discovered To Reflect On

✍

✍

✍

Raising Your Ebenezer

An Ebenezer is an insight, a principle, or a life lesson that reminds us of what God has done - or is doing - for us on our journey through our tight places. What Ebenezer did you discover for yourself in today's devotional? Use this space to write it out here:

Notes

My Thoughts, Insights, And Reflections

_____

_____

_____

_____

_____

_____

_____

_____

Day 6
Psalm 7
Accusations And Innocence - Part 2

"My shield is with God, who saves the upright in heart."
(Psalm 7:10)

Ray Donovan served as U.S. Secretary of Labor under President Ronald Reagan from 1981 to 1985. He resigned in March of 1985 after being indicted (along with six others) in a highly publicized case brought by a Bronx County, New York, grand jury for larceny and fraud in connection with a public construction project. On May 25, 1987, Donovan and all of the defendants were acquitted. Afterwards, Donovan famously asked, "Which office do I go to, to get my reputation back?" Though separated by thirty centuries, I think Ray Donovan (a devout Catholic), King David, and you and I, share a common question: How should we respond when we are slandered and falsely accused? Now, out of the depth of his own experience of being slandered and falsely accused, David models five responses for us to reflect on.

God Is Our Shield. Earlier, in verse one (see yesterday's devotional), David cried out to God as his refuge. Now, David cries out to God as his shield. David asks God to stand between him and those who are forcing him into this tight place, "Arise, O LORD, in your anger; lift yourself up against the fury of my *enemies*" (7:6). David completes this thought four verses later when he declares, "My shield is with God, who saves the upright in heart" (7:10). David understood that God is our shield between us and the fury of our enemies who have created the tight place we are in. And David understood another truth. God shields us for a reason.

This Is A Test. In the Kingdom of God, nothing happens to us without a reason. Even in our darkest moments, God is quietly working to cause all things to work together for our good (Romans 8:28). Responding to his situation and to what God is doing through it, David refers to God as "you who test the minds and hearts, O righteous God" (7:9). From the trials of Job to the challenges of David to our own struggles today, God always has a greater Kingdom purpose for what He allows into our lives. He is a master teacher (the greatest example being the earthly teaching ministry of Jesus). God shields us from the fury of our enemies to make room for us while He

> In the Kingdom of God, nothing happens to us without a reason. Even in our darkest moments, God is quietly working to cause all things to work together for our good (Romans 8:28).

teaches us truths about Himself and His Kingdom. In the process, He tests us to discover whether or not we're learning those truths. Lessons unlearned often get repeated. Why? Because in the Kingdom of God, the author of our salvation is more concerned with our character than He is with our comfort. And perhaps one of the most important character lessons we must learn on our spiritual journey into the Kingdom is that, while salvation is a free gift, Christ-likeness comes at a price, including the price of experiencing spiritual truth in the tight places of life. How is He teaching you this lesson in your tight place today?

God Is A Righteous Judge. The concept of God's judgment occurs four times in the span of five verses (expressed using three related Hebrew words), a good indication of its importance. The sense of the Hebrew is that God governs. And as He governs, God judges and passes sentence, vindicating the righteous and punishing the wicked. God's judgment may not be immediate, but it is certain, "God is a righteous judge, and a God who feels indignation every day. If a man does not repent, God will whet his sword; he has bent and readied his bow . . ." (7:11-12).

In His righteous judgment, God will see that the wicked who force us into tight places "come to an end," and He will "establish the righteous." In the process, He tests the minds and hearts of everyone involved, challenging us to reflect on our own condition. So much of what God teaches us is intended to cause reflection rather than to offer resolution. He wants us to reflect on the truths of the Kingdom, allowing them to challenge our hearts and to test our character. Unchallenged hearts and untested character never learn and never grow.

> Unchallenged hearts and untested character never learn and never grow.

We Reap What We Sow. David understood that our God has created a world where justice means our actions have consequences. In the context of his tight place, and the person who caused it, David expresses it this way, "His mischief returns upon his own head, and on his own skull his violence descends" (7:16). There's a timeless principle here that the Apostle Paul would express again ten centuries later in a letter to a struggling fellowship of believers when he tells them, "Do not be deceived: God is not mocked, for whatever one sows, that will he also reap" (Galatians 6:7). I believe David understood that, like God's justice, the wicked reaping what they have sown may not be immediate,

> Today, if God gave you the fruit of the seed you have sown in your Christian walk, what would that fruit be?

but it is certain. We live in a world today that expects - even demands - a life without consequences, regardless of behavior. When it comes to the spiritual life of the Church, too many Christians expect to reap the fruit of Christ-likeness without sowing the seed of discipleship and a tested character. Today, if God gave you the fruit of the seed you have sown in your Christian walk, what would that fruit be? Christ-likeness, or something else?

It's Time To Give Thanks. David saves what is perhaps his most challenging response (and our most challenging lesson) for last. After everything he has been through, being slandered and falsely accused by someone who wanted to tear his soul apart, "rending it in pieces," David concludes his Psalm with a song of thanksgiving, "I will give to the LORD the thanks due to his righteousness, and I will sing praise to the name of the LORD, the Most High" (Psalm 7:17). Perhaps the best sign of a tested heart, a challenged character, and genuine victory over our tight place, is a worshipful heart that offers thanksgiving to God for all He has done for us and taught us in the midst of our tight place. He is the God who seeks us, finds us, meets us, protects us, and teaches us through all of life's tight places as he prepares us for true life in the Kingdom of God.

O Lord our God, we worship You today as Lord over our tight place. You are our shield and protector from the fury of our enemies. You are the God who challenges our hearts and tests our character for greater Christ-likeness. You are the righteous God who judges and vindicates us, assuring us that those who falsely accuse us will one day reap what they have sown. Father, this day empower us to learn all that You are teaching us, and to joyfully accept the challenge of greater Christ-likeness. In Jesus' Name and for His sake we ask it. Amen.

Reflections On "Day 6 - Psalm 7 - Accusations And Innocence - Part 2"
Take few minutes to reflect on what you've discovered through today's devotional

Insights You Discovered To Reflect On

✍

✍

✍

Raising Your Ebenezer
An Ebenezer is an insight, a principle, or a life lesson that reminds us of what God has done - or is doing - for us on our journey through our tight places. What Ebenezer did you discover for yourself in today's devotional? Use this space to write it out here:

Notes

My Thoughts, Insights, And Reflections

_____

_____

_____

_____

_____

_____

_____

_____

_____

Day 7
Psalm 9
A Stronghold of the Poor

"The LORD is a stronghold for the oppressed,
a stronghold in times of trouble."
(Psalm 9:9)

Our Psalm opens on a note of praise and thanksgiving, "I will give thanks to the LORD with my whole heart; I will recount all of your wonderful deeds. I will be glad and exult in you; I will sing praise to your name, O Most High." (9:1-2). The word "recount" (*sapar*)* was used for literal counting (think about counting the great things God has done for you). But it was also used to express the idea of declaring God's greatness. While our first thought might be that David is giving general thanks for all of the wonderful things God has done for Israel, this moment feels much more personal. David is so overwhelmed by God's goodness and all the *wonderful deeds* God has done in his own life that he can't help but declare them in a song of praise. And he focuses his thanksgiving on two things in particular.

Victory Over Enemies. David praises God for the victory He has given him over his enemies. "When my enemies turn back, they stumble and perish before your presence" (9:3). Earlier (Day 5, Psalm 7 - Part 1), we discovered that the word for "enemy" (*'ayab*) communicates an underlying sense of *hostility* or *hatred* toward others. These were serious "enemies" who intended serious harm against David, and David is thankful for God's deliverance. There's a lesson here that you and I need to pause and absorb. You and I will never know all the things God has quietly delivered us from until we stand in the eternal Kingdom and everything is made clear. Eternity will clarify many things.

> You and I will never know all the things God has quietly delivered us from until we stand in the eternal Kingdom and everything is made clear. Eternity will clarify many things.

A Throne of Vindication. David gives thanks because God has "maintained my just cause; you have sat on the throne, giving righteous judgment" (9:4). David sees God as both King and Judge, seated on His throne and judging between him and his enemies. The word translated "righteous judgment" (*shapat*) refers to God's process of judging and passing sentence to either vindicate or punish. The word translated "maintained my just cause" (*mishpat*) refers to God's sentence of vindication on David's behalf. * Think of these two as describing the trial (*shapat*) and the verdict (*mishpat*). We could paraphrase

David as declaring, *"Thank you my God and King. From your throne you have tried my case and vindicated me against my enemies."*

Reflection. I believe David understood a deeper truth about victory and vindication. Yes, David had experienced literal victory over his enemies, declaring for all to hear, "You have rebuked the nations; you have made the wicked perish; you have blotted out their name forever and ever. The enemy came to an end in everlasting ruins; their cities you rooted out; the very memory of them has perished" (9:5-6). But more importantly, David had experienced vindication by the King in the Court of Heaven.

Anyone who has lived in this fallen world for any length of time knows that the righteous don't always experience immediate victory over their enemies. The courts of this world don't always vindicate the righteous and condemn the wicked. If we doubt this reality, we have the experience of Jesus to remind us. A.W. Tozer expressed it this way, "Our Lord died an apparent failure, discredited by the leaders of established religion, rejected by society, and forsaken by His friends. The man who ordered Him to the cross was the successful statesman whose hand the ambitious hack politician kissed. It took the resurrection to demonstrate how gloriously Christ had triumphed and how tragically the governor had failed." *

> The courts of this world don't always vindicate the righteous and condemn the wicked.

In our journey through this life, you and I - like David - are going to experience conflict with people who are offended by the reality that we serve a different King and a different Kingdom. The values of the Kingdom of God conflict with the values of this present evil age (Galatians 1:4). People will make judgments about us, and perhaps even condemn us and force us into tight places.

As believers, we will not always be vindicated in this life. David wasn't. Jesus wasn't. Paul wasn't. Why should we? If you haven't discovered this truth yet, you might want to prepare yourself for a rude awakening. But if by faith, repentance, and redemption we have been vindicated by the King in the Court of Heaven, then all is well, regardless of the opinion of those who have forced us into tight places. Eternity alone will reveal how gloriously we triumphed in Christ.

> Eternity alone will reveal how gloriously we triumphed in Christ.

A Stronghold For the Poor In Times of Trouble. Expanding on his theme of God as the King Who judges with true justice, David introduces us to another dimension of God's justice, "The LORD is a *stronghold* for the *oppressed*, a

Day 7 - A Stronghold of the Poor

stronghold in *times of trouble*" (9:9). God not only judges and vindicates His people, He protects them. Especially the poor and the marginalized.

David makes his case with several key words. The word "stronghold" (*misgab*) refers to something "inaccessibly high."* It came to refer to a safe place, a refuge, a stronghold, or "high tower" that no one can reach. The word for "the oppressed" (*dak*)* occurs so infrequently (only 4 times in the OT), we can only understand it by how it is used alongside two other words. We find all three words together in Psalm 74:21, "Let not the *downtrodden* (*dak*) turn back in shame; let the *poor* and *needy* praise your name." There are five primary Hebrew words for *the poor*. In Psalm 74:21, the word "downtrodden" (*dak*, literally "crushed") is used alongside two of those five words, the poor (*'ani*)* and the needy (*'ebyon*)*, offering us a definition by association: The *dak* are among the poor. The *third* important word in 9:9 completes the picture. *Trouble* is our Hebrew word for a *tight place*. God is a stronghold of protection for the oppressed and downtrodden, and the poor and needy, when they are being forced into tight places during their time of trouble.

How you and I treat the downtrodden, poor, and marginalized attracts God's attention and concern. As if to underscore this point, David declares, "For he who avenges blood is mindful of them; he does not forget the cry of the *afflicted*" (9:12). The word afflicted (*'anaw*) is another of the five Hebrew words for "the poor," and describes someone who has been humbled by affliction.* God is mindful of the

> How you and I treat the downtrodden, the poor, and the marginalized attracts God's attention and concern.

plight of the downtrodden, poor, and afflicted. He hears, and doesn't forget, their cry. Do we . . . hear their cry? Or have we forgotten them?

David's Closing Reflections. David offers us three final reflections. *First,* David offers a purposeful cry for mercy and deliverance from his tight place, "that I may recount all your praises, that in the gates of the daughter of Zion I may rejoice in your salvation" (9:13-14). David reminds us that God's deliverance expresses His mercy toward us, and our response of thankfulness and praise is what He desires most.

Second, David reminds us that God reveals Himself and makes Himself known through His judgments. His judgments remind us that our actions have consequences, and consequences remind us that the wicked will eventually reap what they have sown, "The LORD has made himself known; he has executed judgment; the wicked are snared in the work of their own hands" (9:16).

Third, David reminds us of the difference between the fate of the wicked and the fate of the needy and the poor, "The wicked shall return to Sheol, all the nations that forget God. For *the needy* shall not always be forgotten, and the hope of *the poor* shall not perish forever" (9:17-18). The wicked who oppressed and abused the poor are forgotten by both men and God, leaving them without hope. Not so with the needy and the poor. God knows who to remember, and who to forget. Do we?

God's love and concern for the poor and marginalized that David expresses in this Psalm finds its greatest expression in the New Testament. On His last day of public ministry, Jesus taught His disciples that how they treated "the least of these" would be a reflection of their true spiritual condition, and an indication of where they would spend eternity (see Matthew 25:31-46). Anything that important to Jesus should be important to us.

O Lord our God, we worship You today as the King whose throne is a throne of vindication where You judge and vindicate us in the Court of Heaven. We praise You for being a stronghold of refuge and protection for the poor and oppressed. We worship You and thank You for Your mercy toward us, and for the many unknown perils You have quietly delivered us from in Your great mercy. Father, teach our hearts to respond with thankfulness and praise, even in the midst of our tight place. Give us Your heart of love and concern for the poor, the marginalized, and 'the least of these.' May how we treat them be a true reflection of genuine Christ-likeness and of our true spiritual condition. In Jesus' Name and for His sake we ask it. Amen.

Day 7 - A Stronghold of the Poor

Reflections On "Day 7 - Psalm 9 - A Stronghold of the Poor"
Take few minutes to reflect on what you've discovered through today's devotional

Insights You Discovered To Reflect On

✍

✍

✍

Raising Your Ebenezer
An Ebenezer is an insight, a principle, or a life lesson that reminds us of what God has done - or is doing - for us on our journey through our tight places. What Ebenezer did you discover for yourself in today's devotional? Use this space to write it out here:

Notes

My Thoughts, Insights, And Reflections

_____

_____

_____

_____

_____

_____

_____

_____

_____

_____

Day 8
Psalm 13
How Long, O Lord?

"How long, O LORD?
Will you forget me forever?
How long will you hide your face from me?"
(Psalm 13:1)

The opening verse of this Psalm sets our tone as the Psalmist asks the question that multitudes of believers through the years have silently asked, *How long, O Lord?* The question occurs four times in the first two verses of this Psalm. Yes, David was serious when He asked God, *How long?* And this wasn't the only time, and he wasn't alone. *How Long?* appears in fifteen separate Psalms, six times in Psalms of David, five in Psalms by Asaph, one by Ethan, one by Moses, and in in two more anonymous Psalms.

So, yes, God's people have often asked the same questions as they have cried out to God from a variety of tight places: *How long, O Lord* do we have to endure shame at the hands of others (rumors, gossip, slander, character attacks, etc.). *How long* do we have to endure those who persecute us (and how long before You judge them)? *How long* will my enemy, who put me in this tight place, be exalted over me? *How long* before You rescue me? *How long* do I have to endure people reviling God's Name? *How long* before You turn Your face toward me, rather than away from me? And, *how long will this tight place last?* There are more, but you get the point (feel free to add your own *How Long?* question to the list). *How Long, O Lord?* is the question raised through the centuries by countless struggling saints as they wrestle with the tight places of their lives and wonder, *How long, O Lord?* But, rather than answering these questions, the writer of Scripture challenges us to go deeper.

The Psalmist's cry of *How long, O Lord?* challenges us to reflect on an important spiritual truth that, like a silver thread, weaves its way through the Psalms: *What it means to wait on God.* Sixteen times through twelve Psalms the biblical writers talk about waiting for God, "I waited patiently for the LORD; he

> God wants to move us from asking "How long," to asking, "What are You teaching me?"

inclined to me and heard my cry" (Psalm 40:1). And again, "But for you, O LORD, do I wait; it is you, O Lord my God, who will answer" (Psalm 38:15). Asking *How long?* focuses on the *length* of our tight place. Waiting on God focuses on the *lesson* of our tight place. God wants to move us from asking *How long,* to asking, *What are You teaching me?*

In the Kingdom of God, changing our circumstances is easy for the God of all creation. Changing human hearts and replacing our fears with a faith that can move mountains is the true challenge. And our journey through tight places from fear to faith is often a solitary one that we take alone with God, finding our courage and strength in the words of the Psalmist, "Wait for the LORD; be strong, and let your heart take courage; wait for the LORD!" (Psalm 27:14)

Asking God *How long* reveals our misunderstanding of God's time and purposes. God has a different view of time than we do. We view time in terms of its length. God views time in terms of its significance. We want to know how long our tight place will last. God wants to know what we're learning about Him and His Kingdom. And one of the first lessons

> We view time in terms of its length. God views time in terms of its significance.

He wants us to learn is the importance of perseverance as we patiently wait for Him to unfold His Kingdom purposes. King Saul lost the kingdom and his kingship due to a lack of perseverance, due to his failure to wait for the prophet Samuel to offer sacrifices (see 1 Samuel 10:8; 13:8).

While we are crying out, *How long, O Lord*, God is quietly and sovereignly at work causing all things to work together for our good and for the good of His Kingdom. Martin Luther King, Jr. once observed that the moral arc of the universe bends toward justice.* That's true, but only because the God Who created that moral arc quietly and sovereignly bends it toward His kingdom purposes.

If we could sum up the over-arching lesson of our tight places, perhaps it would be this: God is more concerned with our character and spiritual growth than He is with our comfort. Our humanity makes us impatient, because we are time-bound creatures who understand that our lives are short and we're all in a race against time. Our willingness to persevere in faith and wait patiently for God to do what He has promised is a sign of a growing faith and spiritual maturity.

Our willingness to patiently wait on God (even for years, as Simeon and Anna in Luke 2:22-38), demonstrates a faith willing to believe that God cannot and will not fail us. Faith is believing that the Kingdom of God is greater than whatever tight place we find ourselves in. Faith is believing that the same God who taught us to pray, "Thy Kingdom come, Thy will be done" is at work in our tight places to accomplish His Kingdom will and purposes in our lives. In our humanity, we cry out to God, *How long, O Lord?* He answers us, whispering into our spirits, "Be strong, and let your heart take courage, all you who wait for the LORD!" (Psalm 31:24). And our spirits respond, *And now, O Lord, for what do*

Day 8 - How Long, O Lord?

I wait? My hope is in you.

How is God challenging you to patiently wait in the midst of your tight place with a faith-driven hope that God has a plan for you that is greater than your circumstances?

O Lord, our God, we worship You this day in the midst of our tight places. Jesus taught us to pray for our enemies. We pray for all those who have caused us trouble as part of our tight places. Forgive them, O Lord. Breathe Your Spirit into us and open our eyes to the lessons of patience, perseverance, and forgiveness You are teaching us through our tight place today. We join with David to declare that we trust in Your steadfast love, and our hearts rejoice in your salvation. For Jesus' sake and in His Name we pray. Amen

Reflections On "Day 8 - Psalm 13 - How Long, O Lord"

Take few minutes to reflect on what you've discovered through today's devotional

Insights You Discovered To Reflect On

✎

✎

✎

Raising Your Ebenezer

An Ebenezer is an insight, a principle, or a life lesson that reminds us of what God has done - or is doing - for us on our journey through our tight places. What Ebenezer did you discover for yourself in today's devotional? Use this space to write it out here:

Notes

My Thoughts, Insights, And Reflections

_____

_____

_____

_____

_____

_____

_____

_____

Day 9
Psalm 20
The "Golden Rule"

"May the LORD answer you in the day of trouble!"
(Psalm 20:1a)

On November 24, 1992, four days after a devastating fire at Windsor Castle, Queen Elizabeth II gave a speech at Guildhall in London to celebrate her 40th year on the throne. During the speech, the Queen described 1992 as her *annus horribilis*, her *horrible year*. Yes, even royal monarchs have their own tight places, their own "day of trouble." King David would understand. And according to today's Psalm, he would have prayed for her.

We don't really know what particular occasion surrounded this Psalm. The consensus opinion is that it probably involved David preparing to go into battle and the people of Jerusalem asking God to bless him and to give him victory over their enemies. That's certainly a plausible explanation, but I believe there's more involved here than prayers for victory in battle.

David's declaration in the opening verse sets the tone for this Psalm, "May the LORD answer you in the day of trouble!" (20:1a). This is a tone of praying for others during their *day of trouble*, a phrase that shows up four times in the Psalms.* The phrase could also be translated *the day of tight places*, as the word "trouble" is our Hebrew word for a tight place.

Six Declarations For Tight Places. What follows next is six more declarations - prayers of hope and encouragement - for everyone facing a tight place; for anyone facing their own personal battle. David, the King, understood what it was like to be forced into a tight place. He had been forced into many of them. David understood that those who hear this song sung in worship would one day experience their own *day of trouble*, their own tight place. His song embodies his prayer for them, for himself, and for us. Out of the depths of his own experiences in tight places, David sings and prays six things for everyone experiencing their own tight place.

Protection. "May the name of the God of Jacob protect you!" (20:1b). Perhaps it's no coincidence that, in the next generation, David's son, King Solomon, would declare, "The name of the LORD is a strong tower; the righteous man runs into it and is safe." He goes on to say, "A rich man's wealth is his strong city, and like a high wall in his imagination." (Proverbs 18:10-11). Solomon knew the difference between trusting God for his protection, and trusting in wealth or anything else. Perhaps he learned that lesson at the feet of his father, David, the Psalmist-King.

Help and Support. "May he send you help from the sanctuary and give you support from Zion!" (20:2). In Psalm 146, the Psalmist declares, "Blessed is he whose help is the God of Jacob, whose hope is in the LORD his God" (146:5). David would agree. He understood his own need for help, support, and hope from God during his tight places, and he prays for the same divine help, support, and hope for others as they experience their own tight places. Our hope in God's ultimate goodness and purpose for our lives sustains us in our times of struggle.

Remembrance. "May He remember all your offerings and regard with favor your burnt sacrifices!" (20:3) Remembering is an important spiritual concept in the Psalms, where it occurs twenty-nine times; fifteen times of men remembering God and His work in their lives, and fourteen times of God remembering His people. Reflecting on David's prayer, what do you think God remembers about you and your acts of worship, especially during your seasons of walking through life's tight places? And during those challenging seasons, what do you remember about God's past faithfulness and dealings in your life? Remembering God's past faithfulness encourages our faith and gives us hope for His faithfulness in whatever we're going through today. While our situation may have changed, God's faithfulness remains the same. And it's important to remember His past faithfulness to us.

> Remembering God's past faithfulness encourages our faith and gives us hope for His faithfulness in whatever we're going through today.

Fulfillment. "May he grant you your heart's desire and fulfill all your plans!" (20:4) During our personal "day of trouble," it's a very human response to doubt and question God's will and purposes for our lives. Think of it as the "fog" of spiritual battle, a cloud that temporarily hides God's good plans for us. Our "day of trouble" can cloud our vision and confuse things we thought God had once made clear concerning our future, concerning our "heart's desire," and concerning His plan for our lives. In those times when we find it hard to pray, we need people who believe in us, who have come through their own "day of trouble," and who make it their personal goal to pray us through ours. People who will pray for us that God will "grant you your heart's desire and fulfill all your plans." Who's praying for you today? And who are you praying for?

Celebration. "May we shout for joy over your salvation, and in the name of our God set up our banners!" (20:5a,b). David prays that the time will come when he can celebrate, when he can "shout for joy," over God's salvation and deliverance being experienced by someone else. David's prayer should challenge and encourage our own prayer response toward others. How do we respond to God's blessing in the life of someone who's been struggling? Do we pray for them during their "day of trouble"? And do we look forward to celebrating God's goodness in their life when God delivers them from their tight place? David did. Let's follow his example.

Answered Prayer. "May the LORD fulfill all your petitions!" (20:5c) None of us can read the hearts and minds of people who are struggling and know what they are praying for during their time of struggles. But we can support their prayers with our prayers, asking God to hear, to answer, and to fulfill all their petitions. When those around us are struggling, they don't need us to filter and judge their prayers (something God does with all our prayers). They need us to support them, to encourage them, and to pray for them the way we would want them to pray for us if our situations were reversed.

David's six-fold prayer for those experiencing their "day of trouble" challenges us with a question: How do I respond when someone I know is experiencing their "day of trouble"? Do I pray for them during their tight place the way I would want them to pray for me

> Pray for others the way you would want them to pray for you.

in mine? Welcome to the "Golden Rule of Prayer in Tight Places." In his prayer, David models what Jesus would later teach, "So whatever you wish that others would do to you, do also to them, for this is the Law and the Prophets" (Matthew 7:12). As you probably already know, Jesus' words here have come to be known as "the Golden Rule." It's a spiritual principle well-known, but poorly practiced. In today's Psalm, David models what Jesus teaches, offering another spiritual lesson. In the Kingdom of God, timeless spiritual truth frequently comes full-circle. And the "Golden Rule of Prayer in Tight Places" is one of those timeless truths. Pray for others the way you would want them to pray for you.

Comfort Others As God Has Comforted You. But there's a final spiritual truth we can glean from this Psalm to sustain us during the dark days of our "day of trouble" (think of this as a "bonus declaration"). In the Kingdom of God, our experiences through tight places are never wasted. This time we'll draw on the Apostle Paul and his experience in tight places. "Blessed be the God and Father of our Lord Jesus Christ, the Father of mercies and God of all comfort, who comforts us in all our affliction, so that we may be able to comfort those who are in any affliction, with the comfort with which we ourselves are comforted by God." (2 Corinthians 1:3-4)

Do you see the truth here? Do you hear the lesson? Paul explains that, while ministering in Asia, he and his companions found themselves in such a tight place that they thought they were going to die (see 2 Corinthians 1:8). But God delivered them

> In the Kingdom of God, our tight places, and the lessons they teach us, are never wasted.

from their life-threatening tight place. And now, because of his experience, Paul could comfort and encourage others in their tight place, "with the comfort with which we ourselves are comforted by God." Paul models in the New Testament what David modeled in today's Psalm. In the Kingdom of God, our tight places, and the lessons they teach us, are never wasted. What lesson is He teaching you today?

O Lord, our God, we worship and give You thanks this day, O Lord, for sustaining us and delivering us from the tight places of our life, and for the lessons they teach us. Empower us by Your Spirit to pray for others the way we would want them to pray for us, and to use our experience to comfort them in their "day of trouble" as You have comforted us during our tight places. These things we ask for the sake of Your glory, for the glory of Your Kingdom, and in the glorious Name of Jesus. Amen.

Day 9 - The "Golden Rule"

Reflections On "Day 9 - Psalm 20 - 'The Golden Rule'"
Take few minutes to reflect on what you've discovered through today's devotional

Insights You Discovered To Reflect On

✍

✍

✍

Raising Your Ebenezer
An Ebenezer is an insight, a principle, or a life lesson that reminds us of what God has done - or is doing - for us on our journey through our tight places. What Ebenezer did you discover for yourself in today's devotional? Use this space to write it out here:

Notes

My Thoughts, Insights, And Reflections

_____

_____

_____

_____

_____

_____

_____

_____

_____

Day 10
Psalm 23
Our Shepherd In Tight Places

"You prepare a table before me in the presence of my enemies;
you anoint my head with oil;
my cup overflows."
(Psalm 23:4)

One of the most challenging tasks facing any devotional writer is the challenge of discovering and sharing some new insight from one of the most well known Scriptures in the Bible. Who in the Christian world (and much of the non-Christian world) hasn't heard the opening words of the 23rd Psalm, "The Lord is my shepherd; I shall not want."

In addition to being perhaps the best known - and best loved - of all the 150 Psalms, Psalm 23 is also one of the shortest Psalms, made up of only six verses and fifty-five Hebrew words.* Those six verses and fifty-five words have exercised a profound influence over the spiritual life of God's people for centuries, and for good reason. Let's spend some time reflecting on how the God Whom we worship and serve is our Shepherd in the *tight places* of our life.

A Shepherd Who Restores (23:1-3)
"The LORD is my shepherd; I shall not want. He makes me lie down in green pastures. He leads me beside still waters. He restores my soul. He leads me in paths of righteousness for his name's sake." (Psalm 23:1-3)

David opens this Psalm with a powerful declaration about his relationship with the God of Israel - *The LORD is my shepherd*. In most English versions, LORD appears in all caps. That's to alert the reader that the unique name of Israel's God, first revealed to Moses (Exodus 3:13-14), is being used. David's declaration isn't an appeal to some generic idea of "god." No. It's a clear statement of his faith in the God of Israel, *"Jehovah (YHWH) is my Shepherd."* What more could David, you, or I want than to know that, in the tight places of our life, the self-existent God Who created heaven and earth is our Shepherd.

David had been a shepherd. He understood how God, like a shepherd, meets our needs, leads us into places of rest and peace, and guides our footsteps onto "paths of righteousness" that reflect His Kingdom will and purposes. David's chief worship leader, Asaph, would later echo David's shepherd imagery, saying, "Your way was through the sea, your path through the great waters; yet your footprints were unseen. You led your people like a flock by the hand of Moses and Aaron" (Psalm 77:19-20). Who is it that leads His people "like a flock"? God, our Shepherd. And He does this not because we are good and deserving, but because He is good and gracious. And because we belong to Him and bear his Name, "We are His people, and the sheep of His pasture" (Psalm 100:3).

The Fear of Death (23:4)

"Even though I walk through the valley of the shadow of death, I will fear no evil, for you are with me; your rod and your staff, they comfort me." (Psalm 23:4)

There is no place in human experience more common or more fearful than "the valley of the shadow of death." Everyone dies, says the Psalmist, "What man can live and never see death? Who can deliver his soul from the power of Sheol?" (Psalm 89:48). At some basic level, everyone fears death. Perhaps it's the finality that frightens us.

> There is no place in human experience more common or more fearful than "the valley of the shadow of death."

Perhaps it's knowing that we can't avoid it or control it. Perhaps it's because we know that death makes permanent all the choices we've made in life and sends us on to an accounting that we're unprepared to give.

A single Hebrew word (*tsalmawet*) translates as the "shadow of death" here (also in Psalm 44:19; 107:10, 14). It carries a sense of "deep darkness."* Since the fall of Adam and Eve into sin and death, the "deep darkness of death" has hung over the human race like an inescapable tight place. In the Hebrew worldview, death was a place (*sheol*) of deep darkness; a place of fear and punishment (Psalm 49:14); a place from which God alone could save them, "Our God is a God of salvation, and to GOD, the Lord, belong deliverances from death" (Psalm 68:20).

But biblical revelation is progressive as it moves forward. God reveals more to His biblical writers as time passes. Two hundred and fifty years after David penned this Psalm, the prophet Isaiah saw a coming day when the light of God would shine on those "that dwell in the land of the *shadow of death*" (Isaiah 9:2). What David saw in part, the Prophet Isaiah saw more clearly.

The New Testament would bring even greater clarity. At the birth of John the Baptist, Zacharias repeated Isaiah's prophecy while adding more specifics. He declared that the time had arrived and the light prophesied by Isaiah would soon shine on "those who sit in darkness and in the *shadow of death*," delivering them "from the hand of our enemies," and enabling them to serve God without fear (Luke 1:69-79).

Writing to the early church, the Apostle Paul confirms every believer's victory over their greatest "enemy" - death and the fear of death, declaring, "O death, where is your victory? O death, where is your sting?" (1Corinthians

15:55). In the words of the 19th Century English evangelist, C.H. Spurgeon, commenting on Psalm 23, "We go through the dark tunnel of death and emerge into the light of immortality. We do not die, we do but sleep to wake in glory. Death is not the house but the porch, not the goal but the passage to it." The Kingdom of God has conquered the domain of death and darkness.

> The Kingdom of God has conquered the domain of death and darkness.

In The Presence of Our Enemies (23:5-6)

"You prepare a table before me in the presence of my enemies; you anoint my head with oil; my cup overflows. Surely goodness and mercy shall follow me all the days of my life, and I shall dwell in the house of the LORD forever." (Psalm 23:5-6)

Now we find our Hebrew word for *tight places*, translated here as *enemies*. David uses *tight places* as a metaphor for *enemies*, people who force us into tight places. While death is the greatest enemy the believer will ever face, there are other enemies - other tight places - that come into our lives uninvited, often forced upon us by other people. Our faith in God's power and promise to deliver us from death - the greatest of all enemies - gives us the assurance and confidence we need to face all other *enemies* and to treat them as a table that God has set before us. Just ask Navy Commander Howard Rutledge.

In November of 1965, during the Vietnam War, Navy Commander Howard Rutledge was piloting an F8E Corsair on his 76th combat mission over North Vietnam when his aircraft was shot down near the city of Thanh Hoa. Captured by the enemy, Commander Rutledge would spend the next seven and a half years as the prisoner of the North Vietnamese under regular threats of torture and death. Released in 1973 as the war was ending, he went on to write an account of his experience. He titled it, *In the Presence of Mine Enemies*. His first hand account as a prisoner of war would become the first book-length account of American servicemen held in captivity by the North Vietnamese. An unexpected table set before him in an unexpected place.

What empowers someone to regard their captivity as a table set before them by God, even in the presence of their mortal enemies? Faith in the God Who delivers us from death. Once delivered from the fear of death, all other enemies pale in comparison. In the midst of such a "valley," our faith empowers us to worship and to declare with the Psalmist, "Surely goodness and mercy shall

> Once delivered from the fear of death, all other enemies pale in comparison.

follow me all the days of my life, and I shall dwell in the house of the LORD forever" (Psalm 23:6).

What dark valley - what tight place - are you facing today? Don't be afraid. Only believe, and trust Jesus, Who has conquered sin, death, and every enemy you might face today. He is your Shepherd through your tight place, today and every day.

O Lord, our God, we worship and give You thanks this day. You are our Shepherd Who guides us through all of our dark valleys and tight places. O Lord, dispel our fears, encourage our faith, speak peace to our souls, and remind us that "goodness and mercy shall follow us all the days of our lives." In Jesus' Name we ask it. Amen.

Day 10 - Our Shepherd

Reflections On "Day 10 - Psalm 23 - Our Shepherd In Tight Places"

Take few minutes to reflect on what you've discovered through today's devotional

Insights You Discovered To Reflect On

✍

✍

✍

Raising Your Ebenezer

An Ebenezer is an insight, a principle, or a life lesson that reminds us of what God has done - or is doing - for us on our journey through our tight places. What Ebenezer did you discover for yourself in today's devotional? Use this space to write it out here:

Notes

My Thoughts, Insights, And Reflections

_____

_____

_____

_____

_____

_____

_____

_____

Day 11
Psalm 25
Redeemed Out of All Our Tight Places

"Redeem Israel, O God, out of all his troubles."
(Psalm 25:22)

Today's Psalm unfolds between two "bookends." Themes that show up in the opening verses (not being put to shame and waiting on God) are repeated in the closing verses, like bookends. Between those bookends David unfolds lessons you and I can apply to whatever "troubles" we may be facing today in our own tight place.

A Tale of Two Bookends (25:1-3)

David never tells us the actual nature or circumstances of his "troubles" (yes, our Hebrew word for tight places), simply referring to "enemies" in verse two. In the Psalms, "enemies" are people who force us into tight places. The word "enemies" (*'ayab*) used here, and in verse nineteen for "foes," communicates an underlying sense of hostility or hatred toward others.* Whoever David's "enemies" were, they intended serious harm. Our curiosity might want to know more about David's enemies and his circumstances, but what our hearts need to know is what to do and how to respond when we're facing our own "enemies," those people and circumstances causing us "troubles" and forcing us into our own tight places. In this first of two bookends, David focuses on the importance of three things: trust in God, not being put to shame, and waiting on God. Get ready to take notes, because David is about to take us into "the school of responding in tight places."

David begins his song by affirming his relationship with God, declaring, "To you, O LORD, I lift up my soul, O my God, in you I trust." David's trust in God has a specific focus, "let me not be put to shame; let not my enemies exult over me." David understands that the goal

> In the Kingdom of God, waiting is an act of trust and worship.

of his enemies (both literal enemies and spiritual enemies) is to put him to shame, and in the process, to bring shame on God's Name. He also understands that genuine trust is best expressed through our willingness to wait on God, "Indeed, none who wait for you shall be put to shame" (25:3). Sixteen times through twelve Psalms the biblical writers talk about waiting on God. Why? Because in the Kingdom of God, waiting is an act of trust and worship. We trust Him to understand our situation better than we do, and we worship Him as the One Who is able to cause all things to work together for our good. But there's more. In the Kingdom of God, there always is.

Purposeful Waiting (25:4-7)

In the Kingdom of God, waiting on God is purposeful rather than passive. As he waits on God to reveal Himself in the midst of his tight place, David is aware that he has three needs. *First,* he needs God to teach him the ways of the Kingdom, ways that are very different from those of the world and of his enemies, "Make me

> In the Kingdom of God, waiting on God is purposeful rather than passive.

to know your ways, O LORD; teach me your paths. Lead me in your truth and teach me, for you are the God of my salvation; for you I wait all the day long" (25:4-5). When you and I are in our tight place of "troubles," do we respond according to the values ("ways" and "paths") of the Kingdom of God, or according to the values of the world around us? Like David, most of us still need God to "Lead me in your truth and teach me."

Second, David needs to know that God remembers His "mercy . . . and Your steadfast love" toward His people. God's mercy (*raham*) is His deep love expressed through His compassion toward His suffering people.* His steadfast love (*chesed*) is God's covenant-keeping love that binds Him to His people for their good.* His steadfast covenant-keeping love means God doesn't give up on us in our tight places. In the words of Corrie Ten Boom, "There is no pit so deep that God's love is not deeper still." Whatever tight

> His steadfast covenant keeping love means God doesn't give up on us in our tight places.

place you may be experiencing today, God hasn't given up on you. He sees you through the lens of His mercy and steadfast love. He sees you, and He's got you.

Third, David needs to know that the God who remembers His steadfast love toward him also "forgets" his sins, "Remember not the sins of my youth or my transgressions; according to your steadfast love remember me, for the sake of your goodness, O LORD!" (25:7). And let's be real. Like David, you and I would rather be remembered by God's steadfast love than by our sin! Two hundred and fifty years after David, on two separate occasions, God's prophetic word to His people declared a coming day when He would not only forgive their sins, but would actually no longer remember them, "For I will forgive their iniquity, and I will remember their sin no more" (Jeremiah 31:34, see also Isaiah 43:25). Whether God's forgetfulness is literal or a metaphor, it highlights an important truth. In His mercy and steadfast love, God is kind to the repentant sinner, to the point of responding and saying, "Sin? What sin?" That is divine mercy writ large. When it comes to our sins and failures, you and I tend to remember more of them than God does. He views them through the lens of His mercy, His steadfast love, and His forgiveness. And isn't that how we all want and need to be seen by the God we worship and call "Father"?

Praise for God's Goodness (25:8-11)

Let's be honest with each other. Praise generally isn't our first response when we are being forced into a tight place. David understood this human reality. But David wasn't praising God for his "troubles." David was praising God for His goodness, "Good and upright is the LORD; therefore he instructs sinners in the way" (25:8). God's goodness is seen in the fact that He doesn't simply leave us to our own devices in the midst of our tight places, telling us *It's your mess. Figure it out and deal with it* (although that "boot-strap" approach tends to be very common among American Christians). No. Rather, like a father and teacher, "He leads the humble in what is right, and teaches the humble his way" (25:9) Lessons in humility probably aren't the first lessons we want God to teach us (maybe because lessons in humility tend to painfully wound our pride). Scripture is clear that "God opposes the proud but gives grace to the humble" (James 4:6, 1 Peter 5:5). But through it all, David reminds us that whatever God is doing to guide, to teach, to humble us, and to eventually deliver us from our tight place, He is doing it through the lens of His steadfast love and faithfulness toward us, the people who bear His Name, "All the paths of the LORD are steadfast love and faithfulness, for those who keep his covenant and his testimonies" (25:10).

A Fearful Friendship

David understood two important realities about his relationship with God: fear and friendship. The Psalms, along with the rest of Scripture, have much to say about fear. Nearly all of it can be divided into two basic types of fear: *servile fear* and *sanctified fear*. Servile fear (think "fear that enslaves") is any fear of people, places, things or circumstances apart from God; fear of the unknown; fear of men and what they can do to us; fear of want and suffering; fear of disaster, sickness, and perhaps the greatest fear of all, the fear of death. But all our fears have one thing in common. They all have the power to distract us, enslave us, paralyze us, and prevent us from obeying God and enjoying the blessing of obedience to His will. Our *servile fears* of people, places, things, or

> Our *servile fears* of people, places, things, or circumstances are the collective enemy of the Kingdom of God, and of our spiritual growth.

circumstances are the collective enemy of the Kingdom of God, and of our spiritual growth.

But *sanctified fear* is the one fear that Scripture encourages - *"the fear of the Lord."* More than two dozen Scriptures teach the blessings of *"the fear of the Lord."* Scripture reminds us that "the fear of the Lord is the beginning of wisdom" (Psalm 111:10; Proverbs 9:10; 1:7). Two hundred and fifty years after David sang this song, the Prophet Isaiah prophesied that the coming Messiah would be filled with "the Spirit of wisdom and understanding, the Spirit of counsel and might, the Spirit of knowledge and *the fear of the LORD."* (Isaiah 11:2-3). The *fear of the Lord* is that unique response of the human heart to the holiness of God that produces repentance from sin and faith toward God, and motivates us to obey God in all that He calls us to do (Isaiah experienced his own "fear of the Lord" moment Isaiah 6:1-7). As the Apostle Paul would later write to the believers in the Greek city of Corinth, "Therefore, knowing the *fear of the Lord*, we persuade others" (2 Corinthians 5:11).

David embraced this *fear of the Lord* as an important part of his relationship with God. And, as a result, he also enjoyed an intimacy with God that he describes as *friendship*. "Who is the man who fears the LORD? Him will he instruct in the way that he should choose . . . . The *friendship of the LORD* is for those who *fear* him" (25:12-14). The word "friendship" (*sod*) describes "a trusted circle of intimates who give advice."* From Moses (Exodus 33:11) to David, to you and me, scripture makes it clear that those who walk in faith and the *fear of the Lord* enjoy a unique intimacy and friendship with God (John 15:13-15; see also Job 15:8; 24:9; Proverbs 3:32; Amos 3:7).

The Spiritual Poverty of Tight Places

In addition to a *sanctified* "fear of the Lord" and an intimate friendship with God, David also experienced a profound sense of spiritual poverty, "Turn to me and be gracious to me, for I am lonely and afflicted" (25:16). The word "afflicted" (*'ani*) is one of the five primary Old Testament words for the poor, describing someone who is *poor, afflicted, humble, and needy*. To be spiritually poor is to recognize our

> The tight places of our life reveal the tight places of our heart and our spiritual poverty, and bring us to a place of humility.

deep ongoing need for the fear and friendship of God in the midst of our tight places, "The troubles (*tight places*) of my heart are enlarged; bring me out of my distresses" (25:17). The tight places of our life reveal both the tight places of our heart and our spiritual poverty, and bring us to a place of humility. Our tight places teach us the depth of our spiritual poverty and challenge us to seek God

Day 11 - Redeemed Out of All Our Tight Places

more intimately, "Consider my affliction and my trouble, and forgive all my sins" (25:18). And Jesus promises all who believe that "Blessed are the poor in spirit, for theirs is the kingdom of heaven" (Matthew 5:3).

A Concluding Bookend

David concludes his song with our second bookend. It's a heartfelt cry for God's deliverance and to not be put to shame as he waits on God to redeem him from his tight place and from all his "troubles." It's a song and heartfelt prayer that we, too, can pray, even today.

O Lord, our God, we worship You this day in the midst of our tight place. To You we lift up our soul. Our trust is in You. Father, do not let us be put to shame as we wait upon You to redeem us from all our troubles. Look on us today through the lens of Your mercy and steadfast love. We confess our spiritual poverty, and our need for a deeper walk of intimacy with You. Thank you for the promise of Jesus that those who are truly poor in spirit are blessed, for theirs is the Kingdom of God. For His sake and in His Name we pray. Amen

Reflections On "Day 11 - Psalm 25 - Redeemed Out of All Our Tight Places" Take few minutes to reflect on what you've discovered through today's devotional

Insights You Discovered To Reflect On

✍

✍

✍

Raising Your Ebenezer
An Ebenezer is an insight, a principle, or a life lesson that reminds us of what God has done - or is doing - for us on our journey through our tight places. What Ebenezer did you discover for yourself in today's devotional? Use this space to write it out here:

Notes

My Thoughts, Insights, And Reflections

_____
_____
_____
_____
_____
_____
_____
_____
_____

Day 12
Psalm 27
"One Thing"

"One thing have I asked of the LORD, that will I seek after:
that I may dwell in the house of the LORD all the days of my life,
to gaze upon the beauty of the LORD and to inquire in his temple"
(Psalm 27:4).

David opens today's Psalm with a rhetorical question, "If the Lord is my light, my salvation, and my stronghold of protection, who should I be afraid of?" (27:1). The answer, of course, is "No one!" It isn't that David doesn't have some serious people problems. He does, and refers to them as *evildoers, adversaries,* and *foes.* Think, angry people who intend serious harm and want to force him into a very tight place. And as if that isn't enough, David escalates the potential pressure of this tight place. Even if these people become an army encamped against him, and even if they declare war against him, David declares, "my heart shall not fear . . . . yet I will be confident" (27:3).

No Fear (27:1-3)

No Fear. David's theme in these opening verses is simple: "No fear." No fear of people, of places, of things, or of circumstances. On ten different occasions in the Psalms, the Hebrew phrase "no fear" describes the people of God declaring they will fear nothing and no one except God. The lesson, handed down by David and many others, is clear. God intends our walk of faith to be one of spiritual fearlessness, with our only fear being of God Himself. A *sanctified fear* of God that replaces a *servile fear* of anyone or anything else.

> God intends our walk of faith to be one of spiritual fearlessness, with our only fear being of God Himself.

Cannibals. Yes, David describes these unnamed people ("enemies") with words that make them sound suspiciously like cannibals; people who "eat up my flesh." In an interesting parallel, the New Testament says something similar, "Be sober-minded; be watchful. Your adversary the devil prowls around like a roaring lion, *seeking someone to devour*" (1 Peter 5:8). The idea behind David's words and those of 1 Peter is the same. But Peter elevates the idea to a higher spiritual level. As believers, we have a spiritual adversary who constantly prowls around, looking for an opportunity to force us into a tight place and "devour" us. Our calling is to "Resist him, firm in your faith, knowing that the same kinds of suffering are being experienced by your brotherhood throughout the world" (1

Peter 5:9).

One Thing (27:4-6)

A Secret Law. David wasn't naive or demonstrating a lack of practical experience, wisdom, or judgment concerning these "enemies." He knew them very well. But David knew God well, too, and understood an important spiritual principle: We become like what we focus on. As A.W. Tozer once observed, "We tend by a secret law of the soul

> "We tend by a secret law of the soul to move toward our mental image of God."
> ~ A.W. Tozer

to move toward our mental image of God."* In other words, we become what we focus on. David understood this "secret law," declaring, "One thing have I asked of the LORD, that will I seek after: that I may dwell in the house of the LORD all the days of my life, to gaze upon the beauty of the LORD and to inquire in his temple" (27:4). Later, in the New Testament, the Apostle Paul would repeat this principle in a letter to a small gathering of believers in the Roman city of Philippi, declaring, "One thing I do: forgetting what lies behind and straining forward to what lies ahead, I press on toward the goal for the prize of the upward call of God in Christ Jesus" (Philippians 3:13-14). Both David and Paul understood Tozer's "secret law of the soul," and each committed themselves to pursuing "one thing" - an intentional, single-minded focus on God. Or as David put it, "to gaze upon the beauty of the LORD." What is your focus today . . . and every day?

Choices. Why is all of this "gazing on one thing" important? Because the practical and spiritual battle we are engaged in as believers often comes down to the choices we make regarding what we are going to focus on. Listen again to David, "For He will hide me in His shelter in the day of trouble; He will conceal me under the cover of His tent; He will lift me high upon a rock" (27:5). David's current tight place wasn't an ordinary *day of trouble.* The word "trouble" here (*ra'a'*) is not our word for a tight place, but one that describes a *day of evil.** As believers and disciples of the Kingdom of God, we are frequently forced to choose whether to focus our gaze on "the beauty of the Lord" and His Kingdom (see

> To choose our focus is to choose our future. To choose our focus is to choose who and what we will become like.

Matthew 6:33), or on the evil of this present evil age (Galatians 1:4). To choose our focus is to choose our future. To choose our focus is to choose who and what we will become like as we move forward. What are you choosing to focus today?

Day 12 - "One Thing"

The God Who Takes Us In (27:7-10)

Abandoned and Alone. Our tight places can also be very lonely places. They can fill us with an overwhelming sense of being abandoned and forsaken(or at least forgotten) by friends and family. Abandoned by friends and surrounded by enemies - both human and spiritual - we suddenly find ourselves alone with God. That's where David found himself in this Psalm. David chose to accept God's invitation to seek Him, "You have said, 'Seek my face.' My heart says to you, 'Your face, LORD, do I seek'" (27:8). In his isolation, David chose to accept that invitation because he knew God was the one true friend Who would never abandon him or turn him away, "For my father and my mother have forsaken me, but the LORD will take me in" (27:9). David's son, Solomon, would one day write, "A man of many companions may come to ruin, but there is a friend who sticks closer than a brother" (Proverbs 18:24). David embraced the truth that God is that true friend Who sticks closer than a brother. He is the God Who takes us in when all others have turned us away.

For many professing Christians, finding themselves alone with God is an uncomfortable experience. But a time comes in the life of the mature believer and disciple of the Kingdom when he or she must learn to walk alone with God, to trust Him at a depth they have never known before, and in a tight place where they must trust God without fear. Again, A.W. Tozer sums it up well when he says, "For each of us the time is coming when we shall have nothing but God. Health and wealth and friends and hiding places will be swept away and we shall have only God. To the man of pseudo faith that is a terrifying thought, but to real faith it is one of the most comforting thoughts the heart can entertain." * Amen.

Believing In God's Goodness (27:11-14)

Two Requests. As David comes to the end of his song, he concludes with two requests, and two declarations. *First,* he asks God to teach him the way or path of the Kingdom as he deals with these people, "Teach me your way, O LORD, and lead me on a level path because of my enemies" (27:11). David needs the same things you and I need in our own "day of evil." We need the wisdom of the Kingdom to choose our words and our path carefully as we respond to people and circumstances. *Second,* David asks God not to give him over "to the will of my adversaries," the will of the people who have forced him into this tight place. Inside God's Kingdom will and purpose for us is always the safest place be.

Two Declarations. Ending his song, David declares his faith in God's goodness, a faith that causes him to believe he will see that goodness "in the land of the living." David believes God has good things for him beyond his current tight place. Sometimes, the depth and darkness of our tight place wars against our faith and our ability to believe in God's goodness, or that He has good plans for our future. David understood, and trusted God's goodness. He expressed his trust by declaring his willingness to wait for God to unfold His good plan moving forward, "Wait for the LORD; be strong, and let your heart take courage; wait for the LORD!" (27:14). Today, are you willing to believe in God's goodness, and to wait for Him to manifest it?

O Lord, our God, we worship You this day in the midst of our tight place. Teach us to be fearless in our faith as we face today's challenges. Empower us to focus on the "One Thing" of You and Your Kingdom purposes for us. Guide us by Your Spirit to make wise choices for a Kingdom future. Grant us grace and strength to walk alone with You when all others choose to walk away from us. And empower us by your Spirit to wait on You with confidence as You quietly and sovereignly work all things together for our good. In Jesus Name we ask it. Amen.

Day 12 - "One Thing"

Reflections On "Day 12 - Psalm 27 - 'One Thing'" Take few minutes to reflect on what you've discovered through today's devotional

Insights You Discovered To Reflect On

✍

✍

✍

Raising Your Ebenezer

An Ebenezer is an insight, a principle, or a life lesson that reminds us of what God has done - or is doing - for us on our journey through our tight places. What Ebenezer did you discover for yourself in today's devotional? Use this space to write it out here:

Notes

My Thoughts, Insights, And Reflections

_____

_____

_____

_____

_____

_____

_____

_____

Day 13
Psalm 31
From A Tight Place To A Broad Place

"You have not delivered me into the hand of the enemy;
you have set my feet in a broad place."
(Psalm 31:8)

In today's Psalm, David recounts the personal distress he experienced as a result of being forced into a tight place by unnamed people ("enemies"). Maybe David is recalling his days of fleeing from King Saul and how God delivered him and brought him into "a broad place." We don't know. What we know are the lessons he wants to pass on to us.

Experiences of distress in tight places and deliverance into a broad place didn't start with David. Stories of such experiences create a common thread among God's people, a thread of gold running through people, times, and circumstances. They unite all believers in a Kingdom tapestry and a song of praise celebrating God's mercy, steadfast love, and deliverance. For more generations of His people than you and I can count, God has worked sovereignly and quietly to deliver those who trust Him from the distress of their tight places, to bring them out, and to plant their feet in a broad place. And He's still working on behalf of His people today. And that's David's message in today's Psalm.

Delivered To A Broad Place (31:1-8)

David opens his song with a prayer, "In you, O LORD, do I take refuge; let me never be put to shame; in your righteousness deliver me!" (31:1). A more literal translation of the opening would be "To you, O LORD, do I flee for protection."

Like David, you and I only flee for protection to someone we trust, and David trusted God. He trusted God to not let him be "put to shame" by his enemies. The Hebrew root for "shame" (*bosh*) means "to fall into disgrace" either because of our own failure, or the failure of someone we trusted. It also expresses the sense of confusion, embarrassment, and disgrace felt as a result of defeat by an enemy.* A prayer to not be put to shame is a frequent prayer among God's people, occurring fourteen times in the Psalms. David's prayer is a heartfelt prayer we could all embrace, *"Lord, I flee to you for protection. Please don't let me be publicly humiliated, disgraced, and put to shame by this tight place I've been forced into."* And all God's people said, "Amen!"

> Like David, you and I only flee for protection to someone we trust, and David trusted God.

David's prayerful song continues, "Incline your ear to me; rescue me speedily! Be a rock of refuge for me, a strong fortress to save me!" (31:2). David uses the imagery of God as a rock of refuge and a strong fortress in order to make a point. To flee to God for protection is like seeking refuge in a rock fortress that can be trusted to protect us. The lesson is simple. Like David, you and I can commit our care and safety into God's hands for two reasons. *First*, because He is a rock fortress for our protection. And *Second*, because, unlike the people and circumstances forcing us into life's tight places, His goal is our redemption, not our shame!

David concludes the opening of his song by drawing a sharp contrast between his attitude toward those who have caused him distress on the one hand, and his trust in God's response on the other hand. "I hate those who pay regard to worthless idols," he declares, "but I trust in the LORD" (31:6). The word "worthless" (*hebel*) comes from a root meaning "vanity" or "to become vain."* It literally describes something no more meaningful than a vapor or a breath. David's "enemies" worshiped and served meaningless, worthless idols, false gods that were no more significant than a passing vapor.

The writer of 2 Kings uses *hebel* to describe the fall of Israel into apostasy and exile, saying, "They went after false idols and became false" (2 Kings 17:15). The writer of 2 Kings offers us two lessons to reflect on, lessons David understood. *First*, people take on the character and nature of whatever they worship. *Second*, false gods eventually destroy all who worship them, just as the worship of false gods and idols eventually destroyed the people of Israel (think, the Babylonian Captivity). David highlights this profound contrast. Idols - false gods - are not only worthless vanities, but are ultimately destructive of everyone who serves them. On the other hand, God is trustworthy. He knows our distress, the "tightness" of our soul. In His mercy, He delivers us from the hand of our enemy who is on a path to destruction and wants to drag us along with them. He delivers us and sets our feet in a broad place, "and you have not delivered me into the hand of the enemy; you have set my feet in a broad place" (31:8). When the lesson of our tight place has served its Kingdom purpose, God makes room for us, and leads us out into a broad place.

> When the lesson of our tight place has served its Kingdom purpose, God makes room for us, and leads us out into a broad place.

A Season of Exhaustion (31:9-20)

Exhaustion. The "distress" of our tight place can leave us physically, emotionally, and spiritually exhausted. David expresses it this way, "Be gracious to me, O LORD, for I am in distress; my eye is wasted from grief; my soul and my body also. For my life is spent with sorrow, and my years with sighing; my strength fails because of my iniquity, and my bones waste away" (31:9-10).* These are the words of a saint exhausted from the fight who wants to remind us that our tight places can leave us exhausted, too. Weariness

> Weariness in the struggle isn't a sign of spiritual weakness or lack of faith, but a sign that we are human.

in the struggle isn't a sign of spiritual weakness or lack of faith, but a sign that we are human. David understands, and so does God.

Alone. One of the ripple effects that added to David's personal distress during his tight place was people, "neighbors" and "acquaintances," who avoided him. "Because of all my adversaries I have become a reproach, especially to my neighbors, and an object of dread to my acquaintances; those who see me in the street flee from me. I have been forgotten like one who is dead; I have become like a broken vessel" (31:11-12). Our season of tight places can be a lonely walk, especially when our struggle becomes our reproach, and people we thought were close to us choose to keep their distance from us. It can be disturbing when we discover that people meant more to us than we meant to them. But, as we are discovering, in the Kingdom of God, we are never truly alone.

Trusting His Steadfast Love. A deeper truth finds us when we are forced to walk alone and exhausted through a season of tight places. David expresses this deeper truth when He declares, "But I trust in you, O LORD; I say, 'You are my God.' My times are in your hand; rescue me from the hand of my enemies and from my persecutors! Make your face shine on your servant; save me in your steadfast love!" (31:14-16).

God's steadfast love is perhaps one of the deepest truths in all of Scripture. And our walk through tight places tests the depth of our trust in God's steadfast love and His good plans for us. How firmly do we truly believe in God's love and good plans when our world seems to be falling apart? These moments challenge us to trust in God's love for us more deeply than we

> Our walk through tight places tests the depth of our trust in God's steadfast love and His good plans for us.

have ever trusted before. These moments challenge us to stand alongside David, and alongside troubled saints through the ages, declaring in unison, *"You are my God, and my times - including my time of tight places - are in your hand. Save me in your steadfast love."*

Trusting His Abundant Goodness. But David isn't quite done yet. From the depths of his tight place, surrounded by enemies and adversaries, and suffering reproach from friends and family, David offers one more declaration, "Oh, how abundant is your goodness, which you have stored up for those who fear you and worked for those who take refuge in you, in the sight of the children of mankind!" (31:19).

Despite everything he is going through, David sings his faith in God's ultimate goodness, and in God's good plans for him moving forward. Is that what you and I sing about when we're struggling? David believed in God's goodness and His good plans enough to sing about them "in the sight of the children of mankind." Do we?

Love And Wait (31:21-24)

It's time for David to conclude his song, so he sings about God's steadfast love and how the LORD "has wondrously shown his steadfast love to me when I was in a besieged city." The tight places of our life are places of two-way love. God shows His steadfast love toward us, and we are challenged to express our steadfast love toward Him. "Love the LORD, all you his saints!," David sings, "The LORD preserves the faithful but abundantly repays the one who acts in pride" (31:23). And he concludes his song with a challenge to each of us, "Be strong, and let your heart take courage, all you who wait for the LORD!" (31:24).

In the midst of life's tight places, the people of God pray, trust, and sing of His steadfast love and abundant goodness. They take courage . . . and they wait. Where ever you and I find ourselves today, each of us is waiting to see what God will do next to demonstrate His steadfast love, to deliver us from our tight place, and to bring us into a broad place. May it be today.

O Lord, our God, we worship You today in the midst of our tight place. You are our rock of refuge and protection, the only true God in a world filled with idols and false gods. Thank You that Your Kingdom purpose for our tight place is not our humiliation or destruction, but our redemption in Christ Jesus. We praise and thank You this day for Your goodness, for Your covenant-keeping steadfast love, and for the good plans You have for us. Father, empower us by Your Spirit to explore the depths of Your steadfast love as we wait upon You in faith to deliver us from our tight place and to plant our feet in a broad place, as You have promised. These things we ask in Jesus Name. Amen.

Day 13 - From A Tight Place To A Broad Place

Reflections On "Day 13 - Psalm 31 - From A Tight Place To A Broad Place"
Take few minutes to reflect on what you've discovered through today's devotional

Insights You Discovered To Reflect On

✎

✎

✎

Raising Your Ebenezer
An Ebenezer is an insight, a principle, or a life lesson that reminds us of what God has done - or is doing - for us on our journey through our tight places. What Ebenezer did you discover for yourself in today's devotional? Use this space to write it out here:

Notes

My Thoughts, Insights, And Reflections

_____

_____

_____

_____

_____

_____

_____

_____

Day 14
Psalm 32
A Tight Place Called Sin

*"Blessed is the man against whom the LORD counts no iniquity,
and in whose spirit there is no deceit."* (Psalm 32:2)

Our devotional reflections on life's tight places have been both diverse and similar. The diversity is the result of the broken and fallen human condition, creating a seemingly endless multitude of causes for our tight places. The similarities are the result of the steadfast unchanging nature of God and His dealings with us. Our tight places embody the practical consequences of our spiritual walk through this broken world. That includes our interaction with people of bad intent who want to force us into tight places in their desire to cause us trouble, or even harm. But today's Psalm introduces us to what is perhaps the most difficult and challenging cause of our tight places: our own sin. There is no tighter place than the human soul bound up by it's own sin. And there is no greater freedom than the freedom experienced as a result of God's absolute forgiveness. In today's Psalm, David sings about a tight place called sin, and the way out he found in God's forgiveness.

The Struggle and Blessing of Forgiveness (32:1-5)
"Blessed is the one whose transgression is forgiven, whose sin is covered. Blessed is the man against whom the LORD counts no iniquity, and in whose spirit there is no deceit" (32:1-2).

The Blessing of Forgiveness. David begins today's Psalm by singing about the blessing of forgiveness. David's description of his own failures before God is comprehensive, using three primary Hebrew words for sin. The word "transgression" (*pesha'*) describes a revolt or rebellion against God's law and covenant.* The word "sin" (*chata'*) is the principle Hebrew word for sin, meaning "to miss a mark or a way." * The word "iniquity" (*'awon*) describes "crooked" or "perverse" behavior. * Why would David use all three words? Was his sin so terrible that he needed all three to describe it? No, I don't think so, although he may have felt so. David's description of his failures is so comprehensive because he wants to leave no doubt that God's forgiveness is as comprehensive as our sin.

> David's description of his failures is so comprehensive because he wants to leave no doubt that God's forgiveness is as comprehensive as our sin.

Whether our sin is missing God's mark or way, or engaging in out-right rebellion against God's law, or engaging in crooked - even perverse - behavior, God's love is steadfast, and His forgiveness toward those who repent is complete and comprehensive. Nothing you and I have done - or ever will do - can place us beyond God's love and forgiveness. In the words of the old hymn, "Grace, grace, God's grace. Grace that is greater than all my sin."

The Struggle of Confession. But for David, God's forgiveness came after an intense personal struggle. David discovered that sin is a sickness of the soul that grows in silence, "For when I kept silent, my bones wasted away through my groaning all day long. For day and night your hand was heavy upon me; my strength was dried up as by the heat of summer"

> Like an untreated cancer, sin grows and slowly destroys us from the inside out.

(32:3-4). Like an untreated cancer, sin grows and slowly destroys us from the inside out. The only cure is our confession and God's forgiveness, "I acknowledged my sin to you, and I did not cover my iniquity; I said, 'I will confess my transgressions to the LORD,' and you forgave the iniquity of my sin" (32:5).

God, Our Hiding Place (32:6-7)

Safe From A Flood of Judgment. Having sung about sin and forgiveness, David offers metaphors to underscore the blessing of being among those who confess their sin and enjoy God's forgiveness. He begins with an image of a flood and "the rush of great waters" of God's judgment, "Therefore let everyone who is godly offer prayer to you at a time when you may be found; surely in the rush of great waters, they shall not reach him" (32:6).

There are recognizable times in our life when God is moving. Scripture refers to these as seasons, "For everything there is a season, and a time for every matter under heaven" (Ecclesiastes 3:1). Times and seasons are those special life moments when the Holy Spirit challenges us, inviting us to seek God. Why? Because judgment - a rush of great waters - is

> God's forgiveness and deliverance from judgment are offered to us on His terms, not ours.

coming. If we don't want to be caught up and swept away by the "great waters" of God's judgment, then we must respond to the Spirit's promptings by seeking God in faith and repentance for His complete forgiveness. God's forgiveness and deliverance from judgment are offered to us on His terms, not ours.

From A Tight Place To A Hiding Place. Using a final metaphor, David sees God as his "hiding place" (*sether*),* a place of protection from the "trouble" of

Day 14 - A Tight Place Called Sin

his *tight place*, "You are a hiding place for me; you preserve me from trouble; you surround me with shouts of deliverance" (32:7). Whatever tight place of sin you and I may find ourselves in today, God is the greater hiding place of safety and protection for the repentant and forgiven sinner. And in that safe hiding place, He surrounds us with shouts of deliverance.

A Teachable Spirit (32:8-9)

Trading A Bit And Bridle For A Yoke. In the Kingdom of God, every tight place we experience represents a teachable moment in our spiritual journey. God in His wisdom never wastes a tight place or a teachable moment. His purpose is always to teach and instruct us in the ways of His Kingdom, "I will instruct you and teach you in the way you should go . . ." (32:8). Our tight places present us with practical questions: *What is God working to teach me? About faith? About perseverance? About obedience? About Himself?* And each teachable moment also comes with a warning, "Be not like a horse or a mule, without understanding, which must be curbed with bit and bridle, or it will not stay near you" (32:9).

> In the Kingdom of God, every tight place we experience represents a teachable moment in our spiritual journey.

The purpose of the bit and bridle is to teach a stubborn horse obedience. And none of us want our behavior compared to the stubbornness of a horse . . . or a mule. But in the Kingdom of God, the good news is that Jesus invites us to trade the bit and bridle of stubbornness for His yoke of obedience, "Come to me, all who labor and are heavy laden, and I will give you rest. Take my yoke upon you, and learn from me, for I am gentle and lowly in heart, and you will find rest for your souls. For my yoke is easy, and my burden is light" (Matthew 11:28-30).

> In the Kingdom of God, the good news is that Jesus invites us to trade the bit and bridle of stubbornness for His yoke of obedience.

What lesson is God working to teach you through your tight place today? Is it a lesson about confessing sin and enjoying God's forgiveness? Is it time for you to trade the bit and bridle of stubbornness for the gift of forgiveness and His yoke of obedience? Jesus wants to yoke you to Himself and to teach you what it means to be a disciple of His Kingdom.

Steadfast Love (32:10-11)

David began this Psalm by singing about the blessing of forgiveness. What began as a song about a tight place called sin, now comes to an end with a song about how "steadfast love surrounds the one who trusts in the LORD" (32:10). His song ends with an encouragement for everyone who has experienced God's forgiveness and emerged from their tight place, "Be glad in the LORD, and rejoice, O righteous, and shout for joy, all you upright in heart!" (32:11).

And all God's people said, "Amen!"

O Lord, our God, how thankful we are this day that You are a God of mercy and forgiveness toward all who come to You in repentance and faith. We praise and thank You, O Lord, that Your forgiveness is as broad and comprehensive as our sin. Deliver us this day from the tight place of our sin, and from the flood waters of Your judgment. Father, we ask that by your Spirit You would grant us a teachable spirit. Empower us to willingly and gladly trade the bit and bridle of stubbornness and rebellion for the yoke of obedience that Jesus offers us, and in Whose Name we ask all these things. Amen.

Day 14 - A Tight Place Called Sin

Reflections On "Day 14 - Psalm 32 - A Tight Place Called Sin"
Take few minutes to reflect on what you've discovered through today's devotional

Insights You Discovered To Reflect On

✍

✍

✍

Raising Your Ebenezer
An Ebenezer is an insight, a principle, or a life lesson that reminds us of what God has done - or is doing - for us on our journey through our tight places. What Ebenezer did you discover for yourself in today's devotional? Use this space to write it out here:

Notes

My Thoughts, Insights, And Reflections

_____

_____

_____

_____

_____

_____

_____

_____

Day 15
Psalm 34
Celebrating Deliverance

"Oh, magnify the LORD with me,
and let us exalt his name together!"
(Psalm 34:3)

My wife and I had been dating for just over seven months when we decided to announce our engagement to be married. We worked for a Christian ministry in California at the time. To let our friends, family, and ministry support team know what was happening we decided to create an announcement card with our picture and a Bible verse we felt expressed our thoughts at that important life-moment: "Oh, magnify the LORD with me, and let us exalt his name together!" Yes, verse 3 of today's Psalm. Like David, we wanted to celebrate God's goodness. But David was a bit wiser and more experienced than we were. He was celebrating his deliverance from life-threatening tight places (see verses 6 & 17). We were celebrating the beginning of our married-life journey together. Little did we know the "tight places" that lay ahead on our journey together.

Most of us will never experience what David experienced in 1 Samuel 21 (the context of today's Psalm), running for his life from an angry and vindictive King Saul, and seeking refuge in the halls of an enemy King, Abimelech.* But life's tight places often come unforseen, unplanned, unannounced, and in surprising forms and disguises. The lessons we learn during one tight place become our collective knowledge and our spiritual insight for addressing the next tight place we encounter. In the Kingdom of God, spiritual

> The lessons we learn during one tight place become our collective knowledge and our spiritual insight for addressing the next tight place we encounter.

maturity is the product of spiritual truth experienced over time. And the tight places of our life are God's practical school of spiritual growth.

Blessing And Humility (34:1-3)

Having been delivered from a life-threatening tight place, David's song overflows with five words describing his heart-attitude toward God as he rejoices in his deliverance: bless, praise, boast, magnify, and exalt. "I will bless the LORD at all times; his praise shall continually be in my mouth. My soul makes its boast in the LORD; let the humble hear and be glad. Oh, magnify the LORD with me, and let us exalt his name together!" (34:1-3).

Like his heart, David's song is filled with thanksgiving toward God. And while his song is for everyone who will listen, David addresses his thoughts to one specific group, "let the humble hear and be glad" (34:2b). As we noted back on Day 7, the word "humble" ('anaw) is one of the five primary Hebrew words for "the poor," and describes someone who has been humbled by affliction.* In the context of today's passage the word describes "the humble poor," the moral and spiritual condition of the godly produced by their struggles and sufferings. They are both humble and poor in spirit. If that sounds familiar, it should, because this verse and the words of David connect us with the words of Jesus, who declared, "Blessed are the poor in spirit, for theirs is the kingdom of heaven" (Matthew 5:3). The poor in spirit, believers who are working their way through their own tight places, are the people David invites to "hear and be glad" and to "magnify the LORD with me, and let us exalt his name together!" (34:3). David invites you and me, and all who "have ears to hear," to join him in the "fellowship of tight places." The spiritual fellowship you and I will find there, among saints past, present, and future, will be amazing and will follow us into eternity.

Deliverance From Fear (34:4-7)

Fear, Terror, and Intimidation. In our Day 1 devotional, we noted that overcoming fear is a common theme in the Psalms (as in much of Scripture). The enemy of faith is not doubt, but fear. In our Psalm today, David rejoices that he "sought the LORD, and he answered me and delivered me from all my fears" (34:4). But in this verse, David uses a different word for "fear"

> In the Kingdom of God, a change of heart often precedes a change of our circumstances.

(*magor*) that carries a sense of terror and intimidation.* When you and I are confronted with what looks like an overwhelming tight place - an overwhelming financial problem, an overwhelming health problem, an overwhelming job or relationship problem - we can quickly feel intimidated and fearful, even terrified. David understood, and he rejoiced that when he "sought the Lord," He answered and "delivered me from all my terrors." What "terror" do you need deliverance from today?

Earlier, in Psalm 13, we noted, "In the Kingdom of God, changing our circumstances is easy for the God of all creation. Changing human hearts and replacing our fears with a faith that can move mountains is the true challenge." When you and I are struggling in our tight place, our first goal is to be delivered from the circumstance. God's first goal is to deliver us from our fear - even our terror - of circumstances. In the Kingdom of God, a change of heart often precedes a change of our circumstances. God will resolve the tight place of our circumstances, but He usually waits until He first resolves the tight place of our hearts. "This poor man cried," declares David, "and the LORD heard him and saved him out of all his troubles (*tight places*)" (34:6).

Camped Among The Angels. Understanding the spiritual reality of the physical world we live in is an important part of conquering our practical day-to-day fears. Just ask David, "The angel of the LORD encamps around those who fear him, and delivers them" (34:7). In the Kingdom of God, when we fight the spiritual battles of our practical tight places, we do not fight alone. David understood this. Do we?

Roughly 150 years after David, the prophet Elisha staked his life and safety on this reality. In 2 Kings 6, we find the king of Syria hunting for the prophet Elisha because he was helping the king of Israel stay one step ahead of the Syrian army. Finally, the king of Syria was able to find and surround Elisha in the town of Dothan. And that's where we'll pick up the

> In the Kingdom of God, when we fight the spiritual battles of our practical tight places, we do not fight alone.

story. "When the servant of the man of God rose early in the morning and went out, behold, an army with horses and chariots was all around the city. And the servant said, 'Alas, my master! What shall we do?'" (6:15). The prophet and his servant were surrounded and in a tight place, where capture (and worse) appeared imminent and unavoidable. What would you do? Listen to Elisha's solution to this practical tight place: "Do not be afraid, for those who are with us are more than those who are with them. Then Elisha prayed and said, 'O LORD, please open his eyes that he may see.' So the LORD opened the eyes of the young man, and he saw, and behold, the mountain was full of horses and chariots of fire all around Elisha" (6:16-17).

Like Elisha, and David before him, we worship and serve Jehovah-Sabbaoth, the Lord of Hosts. As disciples of the Kingdom, we live our lives in this world surrounded by the same unseen - but very real - protection of the hosts of heaven. So, fear not! Today, you're camped among angels.

A Choice Between Good And Evil (34:8-14)

God Is Good To Those Who Fear Him. Having emerged from his tight place of "troubles," David takes time to reflect on what he has learned. He begins by celebrating God's goodness toward His people, "Oh, taste and see that the LORD is good! Blessed is the man who takes refuge in him!" (34:8). David moves quickly to connect God's goodness toward His people with His people's fear of God, "Oh, fear the LORD, you his saints, for those who fear him have no lack!" (34:9).

As we've already discovered, the Psalms have much to say about "the fear of the Lord." At least sixteen different Psalms refer to it in the life of God's people. Biblically, the fear David refers to three times here is not the terror and intimidation we saw above in verse four. This is the overwhelming spiritual awe of God's holiness and goodness that motivates believers to obedience and righteous living, along with seeking God more fully. Such reverential fear empowers both our worship and our walk, with the result that, "The young lions suffer want and hunger; but those who seek the LORD lack no good thing" (34:10).

Choosing, Turning, And Running. In his celebration, David has emphasized both God's goodness toward His people and the importance of God's people responding with genuine spiritual awe-fear toward God. Now comes the point of it all. It's time to choose. "What man is there who desires life and loves many days, that he may see good?" asks David (34:12). As disciples of the Kingdom, if we want to experience God's goodness, then our fear of God should motivate us to make better choices,

> As disciples of the Kingdom, if we want to experience God's goodness, then our fear of God must motivate us to make better choices.

"Turn away from evil and do good; seek peace and pursue it" (34:14). David is now teaching us how to build our relationship with God, and with others: *First,* turn away from evil. *Second,* instead of doing evil, do good (just as God is good and does good). *Third,* seek peace (*shalom*). And don't just seek *shalom* (peace, health, well-being), but "pursue it." The word "pursue" (*radaph*) means to run after or chase. You and I chase after many things in this world, but how many of us listen to David and run after *shalom*? Blessed are the *shalom seekers*, the *shalom chasers*, and the *shalom makers*, for theirs is the Kingdom of God (Jeremiah 29:7; Matthew 5:9).

A God Who Sees, Hears, And Delivers (34:15-22)

It's time for David to conclude his song of thanksgiving and praise. He reminds all who have ears to hear that "the eyes of the LORD are toward the righteous," but "the face of the LORD is against those who do evil." The contrast makes a simple point and asks a simple question: Which are you, and which am I? As disciples of the Kingdom, our spiritual life

> As disciples of the Kingdom, our spiritual life embodies the choices we have made in our pursuit of God and His Kingdom.

Day 15 - Celebrating Deliverance

embodies the choices we have made in our pursuit of God and His Kingdom.

David brings his final point home by declaring that God's favor is with the righteous when they find themselves in tight places, "When the righteous cry for help, the LORD hears and delivers them out of all their *troubles*." As disciples of the Kingdom, we worship a God Who sees us, Who hears us, and Who delivers us from tight places that might otherwise destroy us, "The LORD redeems the life of his servants; none of those who take refuge in him will be condemned." And that's a life-long cause for thanksgiving, praise, and worship.

O Lord, our God, we worship You this day and give You praise for delivering us from all of our tight places. Thank you, Father, for using the tight places of our life as Your school for our spiritual growth. Thank You for teaching us the blessing of humility and poverty of spirit, for delivering us from our fear of circumstances, and for sending Your angels to camp around us to protect and deliver us. Like the patient and loving Father you are, You use our tight places to teach us to turn away from evil, to choose the good, and to chase after Shalom. For all these things we worship and bless You in the name of our Lord Jesus Christ. Amen

Reflections On "Day 15 - Psalm 34 - Celebrating Deliverance"
Take few minutes to reflect on what you've discovered through today's devotional

Insights You Discovered To Reflect On

✎

✎

✎

Raising Your Ebenezer
An Ebenezer is an insight, a principle, or a life lesson that reminds us of what God has done - or is doing - for us on our journey through our tight places. What Ebenezer did you discover for yourself in today's devotional? Use this space to write it out here:

Notes

My Thoughts, Insights, And Reflections

_____
_____
_____
_____
_____
_____
_____
_____
_____

Day 16
Psalm 37
Trusting And Waiting

"Be still before the LORD and wait patiently for him;
fret not yourself over the one who prospers in his way,
over the man who carries out evil devices!"
(Psalm 37:7)

Perspective. When you and I are struggling through the tight places of life, it can be hard to maintain our eternal Kingdom perspective. The pain of our immediate struggle tends to overshadow any eternal answer. I know it's true in my own life, and I think it's safe to say that it's also true in the life of many other disciples of the Kingdom. We struggle with injustice and the apparent unfairness of life, either for ourselves, or for others we see struggling or being treated unfairly or unjustly. Others see it, too. As we noted earlier, Dr. Martin Luther King, Jr. once observed, "The arc of the moral universe is long, but it bends toward justice." The reason the arc of the moral universe is long, and why it bends toward justice at all, is because it stretches into eternity with roots in the Kingdom of God. The very existence of a moral universe is a miracle as great as creation itself.

> The very existence of a moral universe is as great a miracle as creation itself.

Anger In Tight Places (37:1-11)

When you and I experience the tight places of life, or when we see others experiencing the same, especially if those tight places involve being treated unfairly or unjustly, something rises up inside us. Anger, one of the most raw and powerful of human emotions, threatens to overwhelm us. David understood, and addresses it in the opening stanza of his worship song as he sings about our response to evildoers and wrongdoers. "Fret not yourself because of evildoers; be not envious of wrongdoers," David declares. But he isn't done. Three separate times in this Psalm, David tells God's people "Fret not." The word "fret" (*chara*) is a bit more expressive, describing the kindling or blazing up of hot anger.* This is hot, raw emotion. And there's more. In verse eight, it is paired with two more Hebrew words for anger ('*aph* - literally "face" and *chema* - "hot displeasure" or "rage"), "Refrain from *anger*, and forsake *wrath*! Fret not yourself; it tends only to evil" (37:8). A more literal translation would be, "Don't let your face burn hot." The picturesque Hebrew word-play here describes what you and I might call a "hot head," someone whose anger blazes up inside them producing red-faced rage. A very human response to blatant unfairness or injustice, especially when it creates a tight place, either for us or for others.

Don't Let Your Anger Get The Best of You. David's counsel to his listeners is to not let our anger get the best of us by responding with anger-for-anger. Why? Because "it tends only to evil," David warns us. Returning anger-for-anger is like returning evil-for-evil. That's not how the Kingdom of God works. In the

> In the Kingdom of God, blessed are the Shalom-makers, not the "hot heads."

Kingdom of God, blessed are the Shalom-makers, not the "hot heads." The New Testament writer, James, underscores David's counsel when he writes, "Know this, my beloved brothers: let every person be quick to hear, slow to speak, slow to anger; for the anger of man does not produce the righteousness of God" (James 1:19-20). Other than making us feel better, our anger seldom, if ever, produces a positive result. As disciples of the Kingdom, anger is never a solution to our tight places. In fact, dealing with our anger may be one of the very reasons God has allowed our tight place. Think of it as His graduate school classroom for lessons in anger management.

Trust And Wait. So, how are we to respond? In the Kingdom of God, our response to the tight places of our life, and the people or circumstances that created them, is to "Trust in the LORD, and do good; dwell in the land and befriend faithfulness. Delight yourself in the LORD, and he will give you the desires of your heart. Commit your way to the LORD; trust in him, and he will act" (37:3-5). The words *trust* and *wait* appear twice in David's counsel,

> In the Kingdom of God, the ultimate resolution of life's tight places depends on who we trust and where we place our focus.

because in the Kingdom of God, the ultimate resolution of life's tight places depends on who we trust and where we place our focus. Are we trusting God, believing that He has a plan and purpose for what He allows, and are we waiting on Him to reveal it to us? God's promise, good for time and eternity, is that "evildoers shall be cut off, but those who wait for the LORD shall inherit the land" (37:9).

That's what it means to have the Kingdom of God as both our immediate focus and our eternal perspective. In the Kingdom of God, "the meek shall inherit the land and delight themselves in abundant peace (shalom)" even if they must wait until "the age to come" to see it fully realized. In the Kingdom of God, all of God's promises toward His believing people will eventually be fulfilled.

Day 16 - Trusting And Waiting

The Wicked Plots, While God Laughs (37:12-20)

A God Who Laughs. There is an old English proverb that says, *"He who laughs last, laughs best."* It means that the person who is in control at the end of a situation is the one who ultimately succeeds. This old proverb sums up today's Psalm and those situations where evildoers, who appear to be winning, actually end up losing everything, and where God and His people, who appeared to be losing, are the ultimate victors over everyone and everything. Welcome to the story of the Kingdom of God, of our place in it, and what it means when David sings, "The wicked plots against the righteous and gnashes his teeth at him, but the Lord laughs at the wicked, for he sees that his day is coming" (37:12-13).

The Futility of The Wicked. God's laughter does not mean He takes our situation or our suffering lightly. Instead, when God laughs at the absurdity of human behavior, as He does here and in Psalm 2, it's a sign that evildoers and their plans will fail, and that God and His plans for His people will prevail. He is well aware of the struggles you and I are going

> God knows as fact what you and I must see with the eye of faith.

through in the season of our tight place. Nothing escapes His attention. He sees us when we are poor and needy, and when we are being taken advantage of by those who are more powerful. He comforts and assures us that, "better is the little that the righteous has than the abundance of many wicked" (37:16, warning us against envy and covetousness), and that His people "are not put to shame in evil times; in the days of famine they have abundance" (37:19). God's laughter means that He sees the end from the beginning. He sees the eventual triumph of His Kingdom, the eternal blessing that awaits His people, and the eventual failure and judgement of the wicked. God knows as fact what you and I must see with the eye of faith, that "the wicked will perish; the enemies of the LORD are like the glory of the pastures; they vanish—like smoke they vanish away" (37:20). God laughs at the absurdity of the wicked.

The Blessing of the Righteous (37:21-31)

The Character of The Righteous. Throughout this Psalm, David sings about the character of the righteous and how they enjoy the favor of God. Yes, even in their tight places. The tight places of our life test our character in real time, and in real terms. Theoretical generosity isn't a test of our character. Being challenged to share our last $20 with someone in need is, "The wicked borrows but does not pay back, but the righteous is generous and gives" (37:21).

Starting in verse 21 and continuing through verse 26, David focuses his thoughts on God's material provision and how the righteous handle material resources. The righteous are generous with their resources, both in their giving and in their lending to those in need. And when times turn tight, their steps are established by the Lord. If they "fall" into a tight place materially (and who of us hasn't been in a financial tight place?), it isn't catastrophic. They "shall not be cast headlong," because God holds their hand. Even in their most challenging tight places, God never forsakes them . . . or us.

A Blessing That Lasts "Forever." Three times in this Psalm (vs. 18, 27, 28) David describes the blessings of God toward the righteous as being "forever" (*'olam*). The Hebrew word is used more than 300 times in the Old Testament describing "indefinite continuance into the very distant future." It is the Old Testament word to describe *forever* or *eternity*.* David's choice of this word elevates the issue of our character and of God's blessing up to the

> As disciples of the Kingdom, our struggles in tight places and the lessons they teach us are preparation for our coming life in God's eternal Kingdom.

level of the Kingdom of God and what the New Testament will refer to as "the age to come." In Psalm 145, David uses this word to describe God's Kingdom when he declares, "Your kingdom is an everlasting (*'olam*) kingdom, and your dominion endures throughout all generations" (145:13). An eternal perspective on our character and God's blessings empowers David to declare, "Turn away from evil and do good; so shall you dwell forever" (*'olam*). David understood that nothing in this fallen world lasts forever. Only the Kingdom of God is eternal. And David also understood that our choices in this life to "turn away from evil and to do good" have eternal consequences (see also Matthew 25:31-46). As disciples of the Kingdom, our struggles in tight places and the lessons they teach us are preparation for our coming life in God's eternal Kingdom. That's what it means to have an eternal perspective on today's struggles.

A Stronghold In Times of Trouble (37:32-40)

It's time for David to conclude his song. He concludes with a familiar theme, that the tight places of our life are often caused by people. David's Response to the "people problems" in his life - and his encouragement to us - is simple but profound, "Wait for the LORD and keep his way, and he will exalt you to inherit the land; you will look on when the wicked are cut off" (37:34).

David's conclusion emphasizes the importance of trusting and waiting on God, and making choices that reflect the values of our faith and His Kingdom. For David, the tight places of our life represent watershed moments for our walk in the Kingdom of God, moments when we must choose which side of the watershed we want to live on. Our choice, says David, will determine whether

Day 16 - Trusting And Waiting

or not we have a future, "Mark the blameless and behold the upright, for *there is a future for the man of peace*. But transgressors shall be altogether destroyed; *the future of the wicked shall be cut off*" (37:37-38).

In the Kingdom of God, our spiritual lives embody the consequences of the choices we have made during our watershed moments, our personal "times of trouble" in our personal tight places, "The salvation of the righteous is from the LORD; he is their stronghold in the time of trouble" (37:39).

O Lord, our God, we worship You this day and thank you for the moral universe You have created. It causes our hearts to cry out against injustice and to long for Your justice in the midst of our tight places. Deliver us, O Lord, from uncontrolled anger and empower us to be Shalom-makers rather than "hot heads." Remind us of the futility of the wicked who work to force us into tight places. You laugh at them because You know their end from their beginning. Open our spiritual eyes to see by faith what You know as fact: that we are being prepared for life in an eternal Kingdom. In the midst of our tight place today, we declare that we trust You and are waiting on You to show yourself mighty to deliver and to save in the name of our Lord Jesus Christ. Amen.

Reflections On "Day 16 - Psalm 37 - Trusting And Waiting"
Take few minutes to reflect on what you've discovered through today's devotional.

Insights You Discovered To Reflect On

✎

✎

✎

Raising Your Ebenezer
An Ebenezer is an insight, a principle, or a life lesson that reminds us of what God has done - or is doing - for us on our journey through our tight places. What Ebenezer did you discover for yourself in today's devotional? Use this space to write it out here:

Notes

My Thoughts, Insights, And Reflections

_____

_____

_____

_____

_____

_____

_____

_____

Day 17
Psalm 42 - 43
Spiritual Thirst In Tight Places

"As a deer pants for flowing streams,
so pants my soul for you, O God.
My soul thirsts for God, for the living God.
When shall I come and appear before God?"
(Psalm 42:1-2)

Today we discover a rare treat, one song, sung in two parts by the sons of Korah. Derek Kinder describes this song as one of the most sadly beautiful of all the Psalms.* It would be hard to disagree. The Psalmist opens his song with the spiritual thirst of a believer experiencing both a spiritual drought and a tight place. And that is where the Psalmist, Korah, finds himself in this song.

A Spiritual Drought (42:1-5)

Korah opens his song with words that have resonated with believers down through the ages, "As a deer pants for flowing streams, so pants my soul for you, O God. My soul thirsts for God, for the living God. When shall I come and appear before God?" The Psalmist finds himself in a season of spiritual drought, along with being in a tight place. He never tells us the nature of his tight place, only that it involves "adversaries" who "taunt me, while they say to me all the day long, 'Where is your God?'" (42:10)

Feelings of spiritual drought are common among God's people throughout history. And so is the flood of emotions that we humans experience: fear, depression, inner turmoil, hope, and even praise, and often in about that order. The tight places of our life tend to squeeze all of these emotions to the surface and we find ourselves crying out with the Psalmist, "Why are you cast down, O my soul, and why are you in turmoil within me?" (42:5). It's a question we have all asked at some point (or will ask at some future point). Korah will ask it three times in the span of sixteen verses. This drought and this tight place together embody the Psalmist's "dark night of the soul." *

Adversaries. When we have been forced into a tight place by "adversaries," whether human or spiritual; when we are struggling through a prolonged spiritual drought and God feels very distant; when we have declared our faith but find ourselves still struggling; when others can't understand the journey of faith God has us on and mockingly ask, "Where is your God?"; when we find

> Feelings of spiritual drought are common among God's people throughout history.

101

ourselves remembering earlier days and better times when life was good; when our soul is in turmoil and we find ourselves spiritually and emotionally "cast down," that's when the Holy Spirit quietly whispers and reminds us that we are not alone. As disciples of the Kingdom, we stand among a large company of saints, sharing a common Kingdom experience alongside the Psalmist and generations of God's believing people. Welcome to the company of the spiritually struggling and thirsty who cry out, "Why are you cast down, O my soul, and why are you in turmoil within me? Hope in God; for I shall again praise him, my salvation and my God" (42:5).

> As disciples of the Kingdom, we stand among a large company of saints, sharing a common Kingdom experience alongside the Psalmist and generations of God's believing people.

The Depths of Faith And Despair 42:6b - 11)

"Deep calls to deep at the roar of your waterfalls; all your breakers and your waves have gone over me. By day the LORD commands his steadfast love, and at night his song is with me, a prayer to the God of my life" (42:7-8).

Three Repeated Themes. The depths of the Psalmist's tight place can be acutely felt in three repeated themes: Where is God? (42:3, 10), Why are you cast down? (42:5,10; 43:5), and Why do I go about mourning because of the oppression of the enemy? (42:9, 43:2). We might relate to them better if we restate them: *I believe in God, so why isn't He helping me when I need Him? Why am I feeling so spiritually and emotionally down? Why hasn't God resolved my desperate circumstances?*

Simply put, the Psalmist is in complete melt-down. He feels the weight of his circumstances, the weight of his "adversaries," and the weight of his spiritual drought, all crashing down on him with no deliverance in sight. Such raw honesty is a welcome expression for believers who have shared a similar experience, but it is often foreign and uncomfortable for believers who see it as God's job to give them a comfortable and trouble free (i.e., "tight place free") life.

> Comfort and a trouble free existence are poor teachers of anything spiritually meaningful or lasting.

Poor Teachers. But comfort and a trouble free existence are poor teachers of anything spiritually meaningful or lasting. For that reason alone, we need to avoid the temptation to give (or to accept) pablum answers to struggling believers. In the Kingdom of God, the tight places of our life are often God's graduate school of spiritual depth, maturity, and life-long wisdom. How else can we learn the lessons of faith, deliverance, and spiritual stability in unstable times, except to experience them? Experiencing the parting of the Red Sea for ourselves, when all hope of deliverance seems lost, is always more impactful and life changing than just reading about it. Reading the biblical account tells us what God has done and can do. But experiencing it for ourselves turns "Yes, God can deliver His people" into "Look! God delivered me." Such a watershed moment transforms our life and our spiritual journey moving forward. Red Sea moments of impossible deliverance from tight places are life-changing for everyone involved.

> In the Kingdom of God, the tight places of our life are often God's graduate school of spiritual depth, maturity, and life-long wisdom.

Our Stability In Unstable Times. The experience of the Psalmist challenges us with a question: What keeps you or me stable in unstable times? The consistent answer of all the Psalmists is that our faith in God's goodness and steadfast love is our stability in unstable times, even when our tight place includes a season of deep, personal spiritual drought. The biblical writers understand that our call to greater spiritual depth often comes disguised as a spiritual drought, a tight place, and "the oppression of the enemy." The writers of the Psalms challenge the worshiping community, both theirs and ours, to a deeper faith. In the Kingdom of God, seasons of spiritual drought and journeys through tight places serve to strip away any veneer of superficial spirituality, leaving us with only raw faith, hope, and love.

Hope. Three times in this Psalm, Korah tells himself to "Hope in God; for I shall again praise him, my salvation and my God." In the midst of his tight place and the depth of his spiritual journey, his ability to praise God remains a future hope. For both New Testament believers and the Psalmist, our hope for deliverance from our tight places is not some nebulous hope-in-hope-itself. In the Kingdom of God, hope is faith waiting with patience for what God has promised. As the Apostle Paul would one day tell the believing community in Rome, "For in this hope we were saved. Now hope that is seen is not hope. For who hopes for what he sees? But if we hope for what we do not see, we wait for it with patience" (Romans 8:24-25). Ours is a living hope, rooted in a living faith that the God we

> In the Kingdom of God, hope is faith waiting with patience for what God has promised.

trust is able to redeem us and deliver us, and to cause all things to work together for our good, as those who love Him and who have been called according to His purpose (Romans 8:28). Our faith-driven hope in God's goodness is our stability in the unstable times of our tight places.

The Longing Of Every Troubled Heart (43:1-5)

Vindication. Every struggling believer harbors a secret need, an unspoken cry of our heart, for personal vindication. We long for God to resolve our tight place and our spiritual drought, to have pity on us, and to restore to us what the locust have consumed (Joel 2:25). The Psalmist is no exception. As he brings his song to a close, he expresses his longing in no uncertain terms, "Vindicate me, O God, and defend my cause against an ungodly people, from the deceitful and unjust man deliver me! For you are the God in whom I take refuge" (43:1-2a).

As we discovered earlier (Day 7, Psalm 9), the Hebrew word for vindication (*shapat*) describes a judicial act, a judge rendering judgment and pronouncing his verdict. We all want our journey of faith and obedience to be acquitted in the Court of Heaven by the Righteous Judge of all the earth. That longing for vindication, expressed by the Psalmist and felt by generations of believers, including you and me, finds its ultimate fulfillment in the words of Jesus, "Well done, good and faithful servant" (Matthew 25:21).

Standing on his belief that his vindication at the hands of a just and merciful God is assured and coming, the Psalmist concludes his song with a self-declaration that is both a question and an answer, "Why are you cast down, O my soul, and why are you in turmoil within me? Hope in God; for I shall again praise him, my salvation and my God" (43:5).

O Lord, our God, today we worship You in a tight place and a season of spiritual drought and thirst. O Lord, we long for Your presence, and for Your deliverance. In the midst of our tight place, others ask, "Where is your God, now that you really need him?" Today we cry to You for a "Red Sea moment" of impossible deliverance that will change our life and silence the voices of unbelief from those who question Your faithfulness. Vindicate us, O Lord. Glorify Your great name and teach us to declare with the Psalmist, "Why are you cast down, O my soul, and why are you in turmoil within me? Hope in God; for I shall again praise Him, my salvation and my God!" In Jesus Name we ask it. Amen.

Day 17 - Spiritual Thirst In Tight Places

Reflections On "Day 17 - Psalm 42-43 - Spiritual Thirst In Tight Places"
Take few minutes to reflect on what you've discovered through today's devotional.

Insights You Discovered To Reflect On

✍

✍

✍

Raising Your Ebenezer
An Ebenezer is an insight, a principle, or a life lesson that reminds us of what God has done - or is doing - for us on our journey through our tight places. What Ebenezer did you discover for yourself in today's devotional? Use this space to write it out here:

Notes

My Thoughts, Insights, And Reflections

_____

_____

_____

_____

_____

_____

_____

_____

_____

Day 18
Psalm 44
The Greater Struggle

"Yet for your sake we are killed all the day long;
we are regarded as sheep to be slaughtered."
(Psalm 44:22)

Today's Psalm by the "sons of Korah" suggests a struggle and a tight place unrelated to any personal or individual sin, or to any sin by Israel as a nation.* Both the "foe" and the tight place appear to be at a completely different level. There is a greater struggle taking place. And that's the story and the lesson that Korah unfolds for us today.

God's Past Faithfulness (44:1-8)
Remembering. We noted earlier in Psalm 20 how "remembering" is an important spiritual practice in the Psalms. It occurs twenty-nine times; fifteen times of men remembering God and His work in their lives, and fourteen times of God remembering His people. Korah begins his song by remembering and singing about God's past faithfulness to His people, "O God, we have heard with our ears, our fathers have told us, what deeds you performed in their days, in the days of old" (44:1). The Psalmist compares God's past work to deliver His people with His more recent acts of deliverance, "But you have saved us from our foes and have put to shame those who hate us" (44:7).

Korah's message is simple. Our fathers fought, and God delivered them. We fight, and God delivers us. Same fight. Same God. Every generation of believers must fight its own battles, but across the generations it has always been God who gives the victory, or allows defeat. That's what we learn when we remember God's faithfulness. In the Kingdom of God, remembering God's past faithfulness is an

> In the Kingdom of God, remembering God's past faithfulness is an act of worship, and an encouragement for the future.

act of worship, and an encouragement for the future, "In God we have boasted continually, and we will give thanks to your name forever" (44:8).

When The Battle Get's The Best Of Us (44:9-16)
There are times during our spiritual journey when our struggles in our tight place get the best of us. We feel like we're losing the battle. In the light of God's past faithfulness, our present distress makes no sense, except to feel like God has somehow abandoned us to our troubles. And so the Psalmist cries out in the

107

midst of his tight place, "But you have rejected us and disgraced us . . . you have made us turn back from the foe, and those who hate us have gotten spoil" (44:9-10). There's more, but you get the point. "Spoil" is what the victor takes from the vanquished after conquering him in battle. And that's how the Psalmist feels at this point in his struggle.

We all have "foes" who force us into our tight places. Some of them are human, practical, and easily identified. Others are spiritual and harder to spot. As disciples of the Kingdom, we are caught up in a spiritual battle that is more than local, bigger than each of us, and more than merely human.* If you doubt that reality in the Old Testament, go back and read the book of Job. He, too, was caught up in a spiritual battle with very practical and tangible consequences, one that was bigger than he understood, and that was more than merely human.

> As disciples of the Kingdom, we are caught up in a spiritual battle that is more than local, bigger than each of us, and more than merely human.

Korah and the Psalmists sang about their "foes" who were forcing them into tight places. Whether it's Job, Korah, David, Daniel, Martin Luther, or us, we are engaged with a battle that is more than local, bigger than each of us, and more than merely human. The Apostle Paul would later explain this truth in greater depth for believers in the City of Ephesus, "We do not wrestle against flesh and blood, but against the rulers, against the authorities, against the cosmic powers over this present darkness, against the spiritual forces of evil in the heavenly places" (Ephesians 6:12). There are times and seasons when our tight places embody the physical and practical manifestation of that larger spiritual battle. And, yes, it can be emotionally, spiritually, and even physically exhausting.

When We've Been Faithful, But . . . (44:17-22)

In the course of our spiritual journey, there are times when God allows in His wisdom what He could easily prevent by His power. We call those times "tight places." They aren't due to any particular sin on our part. Rather, they are the personal manifestation of a much larger spiritual battle raging between the Kingdom of God, and "the cosmic powers over this present darkness . . . . the spiritual forces of evil in the heavenly places" (Ephesians 6:12). Again, if in doubt, just ask Job. Here, Korah

> In the course of our spiritual journey, there are times when God allows in His wisdom what He could easily prevent by His power.

declares that throughout this tight place - one caused by unnamed "foes" - God's people haven't sinned or turned their backs on God and His covenant. They haven't done anything to deserve what they're going through, "All this has come upon us, though we have not forgotten you, and we have not been false to your covenant. Our heart has not turned back, nor have our steps departed from your way" (44:17-18). The question hanging in the air is one that has challenged believers down through the generations, "Why?" If the people have been faithful, then why are we struggling in a tight place and left feeling like we've been abandoned?

A Broken Creation. As New Testament believers living on the resurrection side of the cross of Jesus, we've been redeemed, delivered from the domain of darkness, and transferred to the Kingdom of God and His beloved son (Colossians 1:13). But the world we live in remains broken and under the spiritual oppression of "the god of this age" (2 Corinthians 4:4). All creation still groans, longing to be set free, "And not only the creation, but we ourselves" (Romans 8:22-23). We still experience creation's brokenness in tribulations, troubles, accidents, plagues, sickness, financial struggles, and a host of other tight places unrelated to any sin on our part.

Again, our tight places are not *necessarily* the result of any sin we've committed.* We live in a broken creation where we still have "foes," both spiritual and physical, who cause us problems and force us into tight places where we "groan inwardly as we wait eagerly for adoption as sons, the redemption of our bodies" (Romans 8:23). The Apostle Paul even uses verse 22 from this Psalm in Romans 8 where he declares, "As it is written, 'For your sake we are being killed all the day long; we are regarded as sheep to be slaughtered.' No, in all these things we are more than conquerors through him who loved us" (Romans 8:36-37). For Paul, the struggle of tight places is practical and physical, but our ability to conquer it is deeply spiritual, rooted in Jesus' victory at the cross.

We Conquer When We Are Defeated. The same Apostle who declared we are more than conquerors would soon die by the sword of a Roman executioner as an enemy of the State. To an outside observer, Paul's death was an apparent defeat. But to the eye of faith, in the Kingdom of God, Paul was more than a conqueror. In a prior generation, pastor F.B. Meyer commented on Paul's use of this Psalm, saying, "This is the lesson of the New Testament - that we conquer when we are defeated." Yes, there are times when our tight place is the physical manifestation of a greater spiritual battle. Korah foreshadowed it in his song, the

> In the Kingdom of God, we are more than conquerors, even in the face of apparent defeat.

Apostle Paul recognized it and taught it to believers in Rome. If you are feeling defeated by your tight place today, remember: In the Kingdom of God, we are more than conquerors, even in the face of apparent defeat.

Rouse Yourself, and Rise Up! (44:23-26)

It's time for Korah to conclude his worship song. He begins his concluding stanza with a metaphor that describes how he feels, like God is somehow asleep and needs to be awakened to his need, "Awake! Why are you sleeping, O Lord? Rouse yourself! Do not reject us forever" (44:23). That's a very human response, and one that many of God's struggling people could identify with. Korah concludes this final stanza of his song with a prayer and an appeal, "Rise up; come to our help! Redeem us for the sake of your steadfast love!" (44:26). There's a lesson here for every believer, one that holds true regardless of whatever tight place we may find ourselves struggling through. In the Kingdom of God, God's response to us in our tight places is always rooted and grounded in His steadfast love, which is the inexhaustible well-spring of His mercy, compassion, and grace toward all who believe. And today, that includes you.

O Lord, our God, today we worship You as we remember all of Your past faithfulness to us. We confess, O Lord, that there are days when our struggle in our tight place gets the best of us and we are overwhelmed. Thank You, Father, for reminding us that our personal struggles are part of a much larger struggle between the Kingdom of God and the domain of darkness. We rejoice that as disciples of Your Kingdom, we are more than conquerors, even when we feel defeated, thanks to the One has redeemed us and conquered sin and death, Our Lord Jesus Christ, in whose powerful and matchless name we pray. Amen.

Day 18 - The Greater Struggle

Reflections On "Day 18 - Psalm 44 - The Greater Struggle"
Take few minutes to reflect on what you've discovered through today's devotional.

Insights You Discovered To Reflect On

✍

✍

✍

Raising Your Ebenezer
An Ebenezer is an insight, a principle, or a life lesson that reminds us of what God has done - or is doing - for us on our journey through our tight places. What Ebenezer did you discover for yourself in today's devotional? Use this space to write it out here:

Notes

My Thoughts, Insights, And Reflections

_____

_____

_____

_____

_____

_____

_____

_____

Day 19
Psalm 46
God, Our Fortress

"God is our refuge and strength,
a very present help in trouble."
(Psalm 46:1)

People greatly used by God often find themselves in tight places as a result of their obedience. The great German reformer, Martin Luther, offers us a good example. His tight places started in 1517 when he posted his 95 Theses on the Wittenberg castle church door, challenging medieval church practices. In the four years that followed, Church authorities attacked Luther with threats, accusations, and even excommunication. Finally, summoned to appear at an Imperial Diet at Worms before Emperor Charles V, Luther was condemned as a heretic and an outlaw. On his way home to Wittenberg, Luther was "kidnapped" by friends and spirited away to an undisclosed location where he could be kept safe from arrest and execution. He would remain there for ten months and spend the time translating the New Testament into German for the common people.

Yes, Luther understood something about tight places. Roughly ten years after posting his theses, and five years after being condemned as a heretic and an outlaw by Church and political authorities, Luther wrote and sang about it. Reflecting on his own experiences, and taking his inspiration from Psalm 46, Luther wrote a hymn: *Ein feste Burg ist unser Gott*. If your German is a little rusty, you might know it better as *A Mighty Fortress Is Our God*. That now-famous hymn embodied Martin Luther's response to the tight places of his life. And as if to add an exclamation point to that reality, Luther wrote his inspired hymn while an outbreak of Bubonic Plague ("The Black Death" that had devastated Europe from 1347 to 1353) was burning its way through his home town of Wittenberg, like the unwelcome return visit of a destroying angel. One more tight place added to Luther's list.

Who Is God To You? (46:1)

Earlier, I offered a more literal translation of the opening verse of this Psalm, *God to us, a refuge and strength, an exceedingly present help in tight places*. It's almost as if Korah, the author of this Psalm, is asking his fellow worshipers - and us - a question: *Who is God to you?* How would you answer that question? I think Martin Luther would answer it by saying, *To me, God is a refuge - a mighty fortress - Who protects me from powerful people who want to destroy me and from a fearsome plague that could easily kill me. He is my strength when I am weak, and an exceedingly present help in my tight places.*

The Difference Between Faith and Fear (46:2-3)

The opening verse of Psalm 46 teaches us that we worship a God who seeks us, finds us, and meets us in the tight places of life. And because He is an exceedingly present help in those life moments, something happens to us. We learn the difference between faith and fear, "Therefore, we will not fear though the earth gives way, though the mountains be moved into the heart of the sea, though its waters roar and foam, though the mountains tremble at its swelling" (46:2-3).

The Psalmist understood a truth we all need to embrace: The enemy of our faith is not doubt, but fear. Fear is the human response when our world - our personal slice of the earth - gives way beneath us, those moments when the personal mountains we had counted on suddenly move into a sea of troubles. In those moments of inescapable *tight places*, Scripture reminds us that our God is a refuge and strength, an exceedingly present help in *tight places*. There's more. In the Kingdom of God, there always is.

> The Psalmist understood a truth we all need to embrace: The enemy of our faith is not doubt, but fear.

There Is A River (46:4-7)

The Psalmist understood that overcoming the fears that overwhelm us in our tight places requires more than mere human will power, more than just us "muscling through." We need the work of the Holy Spirit, and so he writes, "There is a river whose streams make glad the city of God, the holy habitation of the Most High" (Psalm 46:4) Students of Scripture know there is no river in Jerusalem ("the city of God"). The image of a river is a metaphor for the Holy Spirit, who fills, encourages, and strengthens all who trust God in their tight places. The ministry of the Holy Spirit empowered the Psalmist to overcome fear with faith, and to confidently declare, "The LORD of hosts is with us; the God of Jacob is our fortress" (46:7).

Come, Behold, and Be Still (46:8-11)

As the Psalmist concludes his song, he offers an invitation to accept and lessons to be learned, "Come, behold the works of the LORD, how he has brought desolations on the earth. He makes wars cease to the end of the earth" (46:8-9a). The invitation is simple, "Come." How often in the chaos of our tight place we miss God's simple invitation to come into His presence and be taught.

The invitation is followed by *the first lesson*, ". . . behold the works of the

Day 19 - God, Our Fortress

LORD." The God who meets us in our personal tight places and replaces our fear with faith is the God who "makes wars cease to the end of the earth," including the personal war raging inside our personal tight place. In the New Testament, Jesus' disciples would discover this truth in a different tight place during a storm on the Sea of Galilee (see Matthew 14 and Mark 4). The God Who can quiet a literal storm on the Sea can still the personal storm of whatever tight place we're experiencing.

Next comes *the second lesson* as the Psalmist tells his listeners to, "Be still, and know that I am God. I will be exalted among the nations, I will be exalted in the earth!" I have a friend and fellow devotional writer who summarized the heart of this lesson with one sentence, *"Only God can talk about stillness when the landscape of our lives is sliding out from beneath us!"** Stillness in the midst of *chaos*, because God is in control and will be exalted! That's what it means to worship the God who seeks us, finds us, and meets us in our tight places. It means we can declare with the Psalmist, "The LORD of hosts is with us; the God of Jacob is our fortress" (46:11). Martin Luther would agree.

> God uses the tight places of our life to teach us truths about Himself we couldn't learn any other way.

Like Jesus and the disciples in a storm on the Sea of Galilee, God uses the tight places of our life to teach us truths about Himself we couldn't learn any other way. As a result, we emerge from those tight places as different and more spiritually mature people than when we entered. What is God teaching you today in your tight place in the current season of your life?

We worship You this day, O God, thanking You for being our exceedingly present help when the landscape of our life slides out from under us into a sea of troubles. Thank You, Father, for the work of the Holy Spirit to dispel our fears, to encourage our faith, to speak peace into our souls, and to remind us that you are our fortress and our strength. In Jesus' mighty Name we ask it. Amen.

Reflections On "Day 19 - Psalm 46 - God, Our Fortress"
Take few minutes to reflect on what you've discovered through today's devotional.

Insights You Discovered To Reflect On

✍

✍

✍

Raising Your Ebenezer
An Ebenezer is an insight, a principle, or a life lesson that reminds us of what God has done - or is doing - for us on our journey through our tight places. What Ebenezer did you discover for yourself in today's devotional? Use this space to write it out here:

Notes

My Thoughts, Insights, And Reflections

_____
_____
_____
_____
_____
_____
_____
_____
_____

Day 20
Psalm 50
Call Upon Me in the Day of Trouble

"Offer to God a sacrifice of thanksgiving,
and perform your vows to the Most High,
and call upon me in the day of trouble;
I will deliver you, and you shall glorify me."
(Psalm 50:14-15)

As we've discovered, the writers of Scripture repeat certain themes, placing them in different contexts in order to teach us different lessons. That's why we discover the theme of tight places in a variety of different life circumstances. An underlying theme of today's Psalm is a coming *day of trouble* (which we will develop more in Day 25). And, yes, the word for *trouble* here is our Hebrew word for *tight places*.

God Is Judge (50:1-6)
Verses one through six set the stage for a new circumstance and a new lesson. A day of judgment is coming and God summons the people of the earth to be His witnesses. "God Himself is judge," the writer tells us, and He's coming to judge His people. He's about to make a distinction, and He wants the whole earth to bear witness.

Distinctions And Separations. Scripture has quite a bit to say about God making distinctions. He makes a distinction between the righteous and the wicked, between those who are His and those who are not, between those who walk in the light of faith, and those who walk in the darkness of unbelief (see Matthew 25:31ff and Revelation 20:11ff).

But, while God separates those who are His from those who are not, He also makes a distinction between the obedient and the disobedient among His own people. So, with all the earth listening in, God speaks to two groups of people: those who make a claim of faith and are outwardly obedient, and those who make a claim of faith, but are not outwardly obedient. For these two groups, God brings two different messages. One message is about the importance of the heart versus external compliance. The other message is about the need for repentance.

God's Message To The Obedient (50:7-15)
Old Testament Israel has been described as the first installment of the renewed and redeemed people of the Kingdom of God. But with echoes of the parable of the net and fish (Matthew 13:47), God now divides this first installment of Kingdom people into two groups. The first group is made up of

everyone who has kept God's covenant by their outward obedience to the 613 requirements of the Law and its array of ritual sacrifices. But in the centuries and generations since the giving of the Law, the sacrifices had become little more than outward religious rituals devoid of faith and spiritual depth. God's message to this group of observant followers is simple, but profound. *I don't rebuke you for your sacrifices, but I don't need them either. The sacrifice I want from you is the sacrifice of a thankful heart.* (See 50:7-15).

Everything God does is for His glory, for His Kingdom, and for the good of those who love and trust Him. God's message to His outwardly obedient people is both a message of correction (*get your heart right*) and a promise of His Presence and His help. The time will come when they will cry out to Him during their *day of trouble*. His promise for that day is, "I will deliver you, and you shall glorify me" (50:15).

> Everything God does is for His glory, for His Kingdom, and for the good of those who love and trust Him.

The calling of every believer is to live a life of faith and obedience, to give thanks in all things, and to glorify God, especially in the *tight places* of our life. Both our tight place and God's deliverance are for our good and for His glory. We can't bribe God for His blessings with our outward works, our religious activities, or our good deeds (see Luke 17:7-10). Our true spiritual condition is most often revealed when tested in the tight places of our life. The believing heart calls out to God in the day of trouble. He delivers us, and we glorify Him and His Kingdom.

God's Message To The Disobedient (50:16-22)

But what about the second group that God calls out in this Psalm? Among God's visible people (both then and now) there are those who reject discipline, disregard God's words, find pleasure in a thief, keep company with adulterers, and practice gossip and slander, even toward their own family members (50:17-20).

> In the Kingdom of God, the rebuke of God is more desirable than the praise of men.

And because God has remained silent and not judged or punished them in real-time, they wrongly conclude that God's silence represents His quiet endorsement of their behavior. "These things you have done, and I have been silent," God told them, "you thought that I was one like yourself" (50:21). Sometimes God's harshest discipline in this life is to be silent, to withhold the convicting work of the Holy Spirit, and to allow us to experience the consequences of our sin and disobedience, like a Divine version of "tough love" teaching us "tough lessons."

Day 20 - Call Upon Me in the Day of Trouble

But God's silence is never permanent. "But now I rebuke you and lay the charge before you," He declares. At that moment, His rebuke becomes a life-changing expression of His mercy toward those pursuing a wrong path. In the Kingdom of God, the rebuke of God is more desirable than the praise of men. The rebuke of God heals and restores, while the praise of men often flatters and deceives, "There is a way that seems right to a man, but its end is the way to death" (Proverbs 14:12).

The Psalmist concludes his song with a strong word directed to the disobedient, but one that speaks meaningfully to both groups: "Mark this, then, you who forget God, lest I tear you apart, and there be none to deliver! The one who offers thanksgiving as his sacrifice glorifies me; to one who orders his way rightly I will show the salvation of God!" (50:22) God reminds the outwardly obedient that thanksgiving is the greater and more pleasing sacrifice that He desires from them. And He reminds the outwardly disobedient that true faith - and salvation - is seen in the life of the person who "orders his way rightly." In the midst of your tight place today, what are people around you seeing? Are they seeing thanksgiving for God's goodness in your life, and are they seeing outward evidence of faith in the face of testing? Yes, those are two tall orders, but that's the calling and today's challenge.

In the Kingdom of God, the ultimate "day of trouble" for each of us is that future day when God will summon all the earth to appear before His judgment seat. In this sense, Psalm 50 is an Old Testament foreshadowing of that day described in Matthew 25:31-46 and Revelation 20:11-15. That day will come as a surprise to many. It will be the ultimate "day of trouble" for those who have chosen outward obedience while neglecting heart transformation and faith, as well as for those who have simply chosen a path of disobedience. The question hangs in the air, "Which one are you, and which one am I?"

> In the Kingdom of God, the ultimate *day of trouble* for each of us is that future day when God will summon all the earth to appear before His judgment seat.

O Lord, our God, we cry out to You in the midst of our tight places. Use this moment, O Lord, to create in us a thankful heart that glorifies You and demonstrates the greatness of Your Kingdom and Your salvation. Deliver us from ritual obedience, from self-centered disobedience, and from the temptation to re-make you in our own image to explain away our sin. This we ask in Jesus' Name. Amen.

Reflections On "Day 20 - Psalm 50 - Call Upon Me In The Day of Trouble"
Take few minutes to reflect on what you've discovered through today's devotional.

Insights You Discovered To Reflect On

✐

✐

✐

Raising Your Ebenezer
An Ebenezer is an insight, a principle, or a life lesson that reminds us of what God has done - or is doing - for us on our journey through our tight places. What Ebenezer did you discover for yourself in today's devotional? Use this space to write it out here:

Notes

My Thoughts, Insights, And Reflections

_____
_____
_____
_____
_____
_____
_____
_____
_____

Day 21
Psalm 69
Exhausted And Overwhelmed - Part 1

"Save me, O God! For the waters have come up to my neck.
I sink in deep mire, where there is no foothold;
I have come into deep waters, and the flood sweeps over me."
(Psalm 69:1-2)

Today begins a two-part look at another Psalm of David. Today's Psalm, which we will continue and finish tomorrow, gives us a deeper look into David's struggles in the tight places of his life. We'll see his struggle to find his footing, his concern for how others will be affected by his struggle, his response to the reproaches leveled by outsiders, his struggles to find God's presence in the midst of his tight place, and more. In Psalm 69, we find a desperate David who is exhausted and overwhelmed by his tight place, and we'll discover the lessons his tight place holds for us.

Mired And Overwhelmed In A Tight Place (69:1-5)

A Comparison and a Connection. David's opening words in today's Psalm reflect the depth of his tight place, "Save me, O God! For the waters have come up to my neck. I sink in deep mire, where there is no foothold; I have come into deep waters, and the flood sweeps over me" (69:2). These are the words of a saint who is exhausted and overwhelmed by their ongoing struggle.

But to fully appreciate what David is experiencing, we need to compare it with another Davidic Psalm. The opening of today's Psalm stands like an "opposite mirror image" to the opening of Psalm 40, where David sings, "I waited patiently for the LORD; he inclined to me and heard my cry. He drew me up from the pit of destruction, out of the miry bog, and set my feet upon a rock, making my steps secure" (Psalm 40:1-2). In Psalm 69, David sings a very different song, "I sink in deep mire, where there is no foothold."

The word "mire" is the key word that connects both Psalms. This unique Hebrew word (*yawen*) only occurs in these two Psalms, and nowhere else in the Old Testament. In Psalm 40, God lifted David "out of the miry bog." But in today's Psalm, David cries "I sink in deep mire." In Psalm 40, David finds a foothold because God "set my feet upon a rock." But in today's Psalm, David cries out that "there is no foothold." Same David, same mire, but two very different prayers.

Exhausted and Overwhelmed. David declares, "I am weary with my crying out; my throat is parched. My eyes grow dim with waiting for my God." This is very different from the David who declared in Psalm 40, "I waited patiently for the

LORD." In this new and very different tight place, patient waiting on God has given way to "My eyes grow dim with waiting for my God." Why the difference between David's response in Psalm 40 and his response in today's Psalm? Let's consider two or three possible lessons about David's differing responses.

First, maybe what we see in Psalm 40 is David's celebration for being delivered from a tight place, while his words in today's Psalm reflect his struggle in the midst of an ongoing and unresolved tight place. It's a human reality that our tight places look very different in our rearview mirror than they do when we're hip-deep in the struggle with no end in sight.

And this opens the door to our *second* lesson. As disciples of the Kingdom, one of the learning-goals of our discipleship is the ability to take the lessons learned in one tight place, lessons best seen and understood in hindsight, and apply them during the next tight place we find ourselves in (and, yes, it's pretty much guaranteed that there will be another one. Just different). Remember, in the Kingdom of God, spiritual maturity is the product of spiritual truth experienced over time, including time spent in the season of our tight place.

> Remember, in the Kingdom of God, spiritual maturity is the product of spiritual truth experienced over time, including time spent in the season of our tight place.

Third, from David's experience we learn that waiting on God doesn't exempt us from struggling while we wait for His answer. Our struggle during our season of tight places can be physically, emotionally, and spiritually exhausting, leaving us feeling weary, bone-tired, and overwhelmed. And our exhaustion can be made even worse by the responses of other people, "More in number than the hairs of my head are those who hate me without cause," David opines, "mighty are those who would destroy me, those who attack me with lies. What I did not steal must I now restore?" (69:4). When we are exhausted and overwhelmed, the people and problems of our tight place look even larger and more challenging. Problems look like mountains, and people look like giants. It may not be true, but it feels true.

The Return of Job's Friends. We don't know who these people were. Were they long-time enemies taking advantage of an opportunity to "dump on" David? Were they former friends who - like Job's friends - misunderstood David's journey, falsely accused him of sin (or gossiped falsely about him, which is also sin), and offered conventional narratives that simply didn't apply, "You've obviously sinned, and your tight place is the result. Confess your sin, change what you're doing, and God will restore you." Sometimes, the most hurtful responses to our tight places come from well-intended friends and fellow believers who misunderstand our journey. In the Kingdom of God, our calling is to encourage faith and to inspire hope in the lives of other believers who are struggling through their tight places. And that was something Job's friends simply didn't know how to do. In the New Testament, the Apostle Paul develops this thought more completely, describing himself

> In the Kingdom of God, our calling is to inspire hope and to encourage faith in the lives of believers who are struggling through their tight places.

as "as a spectacle to the world, to angels, and to men" (1 Corinthians 4:9) In whatever tight place you and I are experiencing, we are a testimony of Jesus and His Kingdom "to the world, to angels, and to men." Your tight place has quite the audience.

Reproach And Reflection (69:6-12)

Our Impact On Others. David is concerned with how others will be impacted by his tight place and how he deals with it, "Let not those who hope in you be put to shame through me, O Lord GOD of hosts; let not those who seek you be brought to dishonor through me, O God of Israel" (69:6). David doesn't want

> As disciples of the Kingdom, we share the reproach that unbelievers level at God, at Jesus, and at the Kingdom of God.

fellow believers - "those who hope in you" - to be discouraged, disgraced, or dishonored because of what he is going through. David also understands that a significant part of his tight place, and the reproaches that he is experiencing from others, is the result of his walk with God, "For zeal for your house has consumed me, and the reproaches of those who reproach you have fallen on me" (69:9). The word "reproach" (*cherpa*) occurs five times in this Psalm with the idea of casting blame or scorn on someone resulting in disgrace or dishonor.* As disciples of the Kingdom, we share the reproach that unbelievers level at God, at Jesus, and at the Kingdom of God. Some people aren't really angry at us, although we may be the immediate target of their anger and reproach. They're actually angry at God and at His Kingdom which we represent. It's how religious leaders and their followers responded to Jesus, and for basically the same reason.

A Time For Reflection. David takes a moment to reflect on how others have responded to his spiritual walk and lifestyle, "When I wept and humbled my soul with fasting, it became my reproach. When I made sackcloth my clothing, I became a byword to them. I am the talk of those who sit in the gate, and the drunkards make songs about me" (69:10-12).

David's reflection highlights a challenging reality faced by every serious disciple of the Kingdom. His spiritual journey and lifestyle have become a reproach to others. He is mocked for it, and "the drunkards make songs about me." Rejection by others over our faith, our convictions, and our lifestyle can be personally painful, especially when we discover that certain people meant more to us than we meant to them. It's a very human reality each of us has to come to terms with. Not everyone we care about will understand our journey through our tight place, and we need to be at peace with that reality.

I once heard a speaker observe that everyone is a fool for something in someone else's eyes, so it's best to be a fool for Christ and to let the chips fall where they will. I think David would agree, especially as it applies to how we deal with the tight places of our life. As believers, our lifestyle *should* be different, not because we're fools, but because we serve a different King, and we serve a different Kingdom.

O Lord, our God, exhausted and overwhelmed, we cry out to You today from the midst of our tight places. You are the God of all our tight places, and we worship You. Today we struggle to apply Your past lessons to our present tight place. Forgive us, O Lord, if we have been slow to learn, and even slower to apply those lessons and to encourage those around us who are also struggling in their tight places. Empower us by Your Spirit to inspire faith, hope, and encouragement in the hearts of those around us who are struggling. And strengthen Your people against those who think we are fools for trusting You, and for serving a different King and serving a different Kingdom. For Jesus' sake and in His Name we ask it. Amen.

Reflections On "Day 21 - Psalm 69 - Exhausted and Overwhelmed - Part 1"
Take few minutes to reflect on what you've discovered through today's devotional.

Insights You Discovered To Reflect On

✍

✍

✍

Raising Your Ebenezer
An Ebenezer is an insight, a principle, or a life lesson that reminds us of what God has done - or is doing - for us on our journey through our tight places. What Ebenezer did you discover for yourself in today's devotional? Use this space to write it out here:

Notes

My Thoughts, Insights, And Reflections

_____

_____

_____

_____

_____

_____

_____

_____

_____

Day 22
Psalm 69
Exhausted And Overwhelmed - Part 2

"But as for me, my prayer is to you, O LORD. At an acceptable time, O God, in the abundance of your steadfast love answer me in your saving faithfulness. Deliver me from sinking in the mire; let me be delivered from my enemies and from the deep waters" (Psalm 69:13-14).

Today we finish the journey through Psalm 69 that we started yesterday. Today David will deal with a wide range of challenges we have all wrestled with in our own season of tight places. Questions like, Do you believe that your tight place is in God's hands, or in yours? Are you trusting Him for His timing? Do you trust His steadfast love and faithfulness to meet your needs and to bring you through it? There's more. In the Kingdom of God, there always is.

Our Tight Places Are In God's Hands (69:13-21)

Timing, Love, and Faithfulness. In the midst of his tight place, David came to better understand how his tight place (and ours) is fully in God's hands. In the process, David discovered important truths about God's timing, His love, and His faithfulness. "But as for me, my prayer is to you, O LORD. At an acceptable time, O God, in the abundance of your steadfast love answer me in your saving faithfulness. Deliver me from sinking in the mire; let me be delivered from my enemies and from the deep waters" (69:13-14).

Like David, you and I would prefer to see God resolve our tight place on our schedule, "sooner rather than later." But David came to understand that God's dealings are always "at an acceptable time." As a friend of mine likes to say, *"God is never late. But He passes up many opportunities to be early."*

The Kingdom of God operates on a different schedule than we do. As the writer of Ecclesiastes says, "For everything there is a season, and a time for every matter under heaven" (Ecclesiastes 3:1). In the New Testament, Paul could confidently declare to

> The Kingdom of God operates on a different schedule than we do.

believers in Galatia, "But when *the fullness of time* had come, God sent forth his Son, born of a woman, born under the law, to redeem those who were under the law, so that we might receive adoption as sons" (Galatians 4:4-5). David reminds us that God's timing for addressing and resolving our tight places is rooted in His steadfast love and faithfulness. He loves us. He is faithful to do all He has promised us. And we can trust Him for His timing to resolve whatever tight place we may be experiencing.

When It Feels Like God Is Hiding From Us. David expresses a feeling we have all experienced at one time or another. Like you and me, struggling through a difficult time, David wonders if God is hiding Himself, "Hide not your face from your servant, for I am in distress; make haste to answer me. Draw near to my soul, redeem me; ransom me because of my enemies!" (69:17-18). And, yes, the word "distress" here is our Hebrew word for a tight place. When you and I are hurting and struggling through our tight places, we long - even "thirst" - for a sense of God's presence. When that sense of His presence is absent for an extended period of time, it can feel like God is hiding Himself from us. And that's how David feels at this moment. The distress and exhaustion of his tight place causes David to cry out and ask God not to hide Himself, but to "draw near to my soul" (On Day 29 we'll address the idea of God hiding Himself in more depth).

God Knows Us And Them. David offers us another morsel of truth that we often forget, "You know my reproach, and my shame and my dishonor; my foes are all known to you" (69:19). You and I tend to overestimate our problems and underestimate God's understanding of the people, problems, and circumstances facing us. He knows the shame and embarrassment that we may be experiencing as a result of what we're going through. And He knows every person who may have been part of forcing us into our tight place, along with the despair we have felt when they and others failed to show pity or to comfort us. He knows.

> You and I tend to overestimate our problems and underestimate God's understanding of the people, problems, and circumstances facing us.

An Imprecatory Prayer (69:22-28)

If God knows every person who has contributed to our tight place, then how should we respond to them? David responds with what has become known as an "imprecatory" prayer, one that calls on God to respond and to judge the person accordingly, "Add to them punishment upon punishment; may they have no acquittal from you. Let them be blotted out of the book of the living; let them not be enrolled among the righteous" (69:27-28). There's more, but you get the point. Some twenty-two Psalms include examples of imprecatory prayers. David's response to people forcing him into his tight place was to pray for them and to put them in God's hands. And that is the basic meaning of an "imprecatory" prayer. We discover a similar response in the life of the prophet Jeremiah, who prayed, "But, O LORD of hosts, who judges righteously, who tests the heart and the mind, let me see your vengeance upon them, for to you have I committed my cause" (Jeremiah 11:19-20).

Before we conclude that David's response (and Jeremiah's) is overly harsh or even "unbiblical," the New Testament has examples of similar responses. The Apostle Paul cautions believers in Corinth, "If anyone has no love for the Lord, let him be accursed. Our Lord, come!" (1 Corinthians 16:22). He sends a more personal warning to his young disciple, Timothy, "Alexander the coppersmith did me great harm; the Lord will repay him according to his deeds. Beware of him yourself, for he strongly opposed our message" (2 Timothy 4:14-15). Responding to people who hurt us by turning them over to God in prayer for Him to deal with is a biblical option within a larger biblical context, "If possible, so far as it depends on you, live peaceably with all. Beloved, never avenge yourselves, but leave it to the wrath of God, for it is written, 'Vengeance is mine, I will repay, says the Lord.' To the contrary, 'if your enemy is hungry, feed him; if he is thirsty, give him something to drink; for by so doing you will heap burning coals on his head.' Do not be overcome by evil, but overcome evil with good" (Romans 12:18-21). In this passage, Paul combines David's imprecatory prayer approach with the "Love your enemies and pray for those who persecute you" teachings of Jesus (Matthew 5:44). Today, turn your people problems over to God in prayer. Let Him deal with them, while you devote yourself to acts of faith, hope, and love.

> Today, turn your people problems over to God in prayer for Him to deal with, and devote yourself to acts of love and kindness.

The Humble Will See It And Be Glad (69:29-36)

David's song is coming to a conclusion. And in spite of the pain of his unresolved tight place, and the people who forced him into it, David chooses to end his song on a note of praise, "I will praise the name of God with a song; I will magnify him with thanksgiving" (Psalm 69:30). Keenly aware that many eyes are watching how he responds, David chooses a response that honors God and encourages those around him, "When the humble see it they will be glad; you who seek God, let your hearts revive. For the LORD hears the needy and does not despise his own people who are prisoners. Let heaven and earth praise him, the seas and everything that moves in them" (69:32-34).

What are you praising God for in the midst of your tight place today, and who is being impacted and encouraged by your example?

O Lord, our God, You are the sovereign God over the tight places of our life, and our times are in Your hands. We wait and long for that acceptable time when You will answer our prayers and deliver us. Thank You that You do not hide Your face from us in our times of distress. Thank You that You know and understand everything we are going through. This day we pray for all those who have contributed to our struggles. Father, we place them in Your hands for You to deal with according to Your Kingdom will and purposes. For our part, we offer up a song of praise and thanksgiving, and ask that You make us an example of Your love and faithfulness to all who are watching our journey. For Jesus' sake and in His Name we ask it. Amen.

Reflections On "Day 22 - Psalm 69 - Exhausted and Overwhelmed - Part 2"
Take few minutes to reflect on what you've discovered through today's devotional.

Insights You Discovered To Reflect On

✍

✍

✍

Raising Your Ebenezer
An Ebenezer is an insight, a principle, or a life lesson that reminds us of what God has done - or is doing - for us on our journey through our tight places. What Ebenezer did you discover for yourself in today's devotional? Use this space to write it out here:

Notes

My Thoughts, Insights, And Reflections

_____
_____
_____
_____
_____
_____
_____
_____

Day 23
Psalm 71
From Youth To Old Age

"O God, from my youth you have taught me,
and I still proclaim your wondrous deeds.
So even to old age and gray hairs, O God, do not forsake me,
until I proclaim your might to another generation,
your power to all those to come."
(Psalm 71:17-18)

In today's Psalm we meet an anonymous worshiping saint whose song expresses his personal reflections on his spiritual journey from youth to old age through many tight places. The blessing of old age, when matched with spiritual maturity, is perspective and the ability to see God's faithfulness over time, fulfilling His promises to us. With the benefit of perspective, we see how the tight places of our life have challenged what we truly believe about God,

> How we live out our spiritual journey and respond to our tight places are the ultimate expression of what we truly believe.

His word, His promises to us, His faithfulness, and more. We see that the tight places of our life are the crucible where God tests us and forces us to examine what we truly believe, and whether or not we're willing to stake our past, our present, and our future on it. As A.W. Tozer once observed, ". . . it might shock some of us profoundly if we were brought suddenly face-to-face with our beliefs and forced to test them in the fires of practical living."* How we live out our spiritual journey and respond to our tight places are the ultimate expression of what we truly believe.

My Rock And My Fortress (71:1-3)
Reflecting the thoughts and prayers of David from the opening verses of an earlier Psalm (Day 13, Psalm 31), our Psalmist has lessons he wants to pass on, starting with the reality that the LORD truly is, and always has been, our refuge, our rock, and our fortress.

Lessons, Not Shame. One of the early lessons the Psalmist sings about has to do with God's purposes for our season of tight places. God's purpose isn't to shame us, "In you, O LORD, do I take refuge; let me never be put to shame!" (71:1). In the Kingdom of God, His purpose is to teach us lessons that we could not learn any other way. Our tight places become our teachable moments.

A Righteous Deliverance. One of the most important lessons you and I will

133

learn from our seasons of tight places has to do with God's righteousness. In the context of today's Psalm, God's righteousness is His faithfulness to keep and fulfill His promises to us. In His righteousness, God will deliver us from our tight places because He has promised to save and keep us. And God is always faithful to His promises. Understanding God's faithfulness enables the Psalmist to sing with confidence, "In your righteousness deliver me and rescue me; incline your ear to me, and save me!" (71:2).

Our Refuge Continually. The Psalmist also wants us to know that, however we describe Him (a rock, refuge, fortress), God's Presence is a place where we can continually come and find refuge, "Be to me a rock of refuge, to which I may continually come" (71:3a). We can only wonder how many times, and on how many occasions, the Psalmist had fled to God for comfort and protection during his life. But he wants us to know that God never grows tired of us seeking refuge in His care. He is "a rock of refuge, to which [we] may *continually* come."

A Command Already Given. Looking back with the perspective of time, experience, and old age, the Psalmist sees God's sovereign hand at work throughout his life, "you have given the command to save me, for you are my rock and my fortress" (71:3b). Whatever you and I may be going through in our season of tight places, we can be at peace knowing that God has gone before us and has already given the command to save us. God is at work quietly and sovereignly turning the *chaos* of our life and our tight places into the *cosmos* of His order, and He calls us to trust Him in the process.

> God is at work quietly and sovereignly turning the chaos of our life into the cosmos of His order, and He calls us to trust Him in the process.

My Hope Since Birth (71:4-6)

Faithfulness And Hope. As the Psalmist's song progresses, more lessons unfold. As we saw earlier, from the perspective of the Psalmist, his deliverance "from the hand of the wicked" has been the result of God's faithfulness to fulfill His promises. Reflecting over the years of his spiritual journey, starting "from before my birth," the Psalmist declares that God's faithfulness has given him *hope*, "For you, O Lord, are my *hope*, my trust, O LORD, from my youth. Upon you I have leaned from before my birth; you are he who took me from my mother's womb. My praise is continually of you" (71:5-6). In the Kingdom of God, hope is faith waiting with patience for what God has promised.

Each of us has a story that is bigger than we know, one that God has been building since before we were born as He prepares us for life both now and in His future Kingdom. The beauty and scope of the story God has been building and continues to build in each of us should cause us to declare with the Psalmist, "My praise is continually of you" (71:6c).

In The Time Of Old Age (71:7-16)

Visible And Vulnerable. The Psalmist has reached a point on his spiritual journey where he feels both visible and vulnerable, declaring, "I have been as a portent to many, but you are my strong refuge" (71:7). The Hebrew word for "portent" (*mopet*) communicates the idea of a miraculous sign.* It's used for Moses' rod changing into a snake (Exodus 7:9), and for the ten plagues God released on the Egyptians. All very visible portents or signs of God's handiwork for others to see and be awestruck by God's dealings. That's how the Psalmist sees himself, and how he feels about God's work to deliver him from his tight places. "My mouth is filled with your praise," he declares, "and with your glory all the day" (71:8). Yes, there's a lesson here for us, too. In our journey through life's tight places, God is at work, both for us and in us. As others watch God work in our lives, they learn what God can do for those who trust Him. Like the Psalmist, you and I are visible portents - signs - for the work of the Kingdom. What are those around you learning about the Kingdom from watching you?

> What are those around you learning about the Kingdom from watching you?

But the Psalmist also feels vulnerable, "Do not cast me off in the time of old age; forsake me not when my strength is spent" (71:9). The aging process slowly robs us of things we have come to trust: health, reflexes, physical strength, mental sharpness, and more, in a process poetically described by the author of Ecclesiastes (12:1-8). The practical result in old age is a deep sense of vulnerability at no longer having the ability to defend ourselves when others try to force us into tight places, "For my enemies speak concerning me; those who watch for my life consult together and say, 'God has forsaken him; pursue and seize him, for there is none to deliver him'" (71:10-11).

Continual Hope and Praise. The Psalmist may feel vulnerable, but he is not hopeless. With years of experience comes wisdom, and the aging Psalmist draws on his years of walking with God to offer wise responses to those who would try to force him into a tight place. He begins by calling out to God for help, "O God, be not far from me; O my God, make haste to help me!" (71:12). In old age, the Psalmist knows where his true strength and help come from. The Psalmist prays that God would "turn the tables" on his enemies and heap on them what they had planned for him, "May my accusers be put to shame and consumed; with scorn and disgrace may they be covered who seek my hurt" (71:13). Next, he chooses continual hope and praise, which probably was not the response his accusers were expecting, "But I will hope continually and will praise you yet more and more" (71:14).

Finally, the Psalmist chooses to talk, not about his troubles, but about God's past "righteous acts" and "deeds of salvation," declaring concerning his enemies, " I will remind them of your righteousness, yours alone" (71:15-16). As a disciple of the Kingdom, when in doubt about the future, remember what God has done for you in the past. And when others question your walk of faith, remind them of what God has done for you. He hasn't changed, but you have grown.

> As a disciple of the Kingdom, when in doubt about the future, remember what God has done for you in the past.

Proclaiming To Another Generation (71:17-21)

He Teaches, and We Proclaim. The Psalmist sees a pattern and purpose in God's dealings through the tight places of his life, "O God, from my youth you have taught me, and I still proclaim your wondrous deeds" (71:17). Through all he has experienced from youth til old age, the Psalmist sees how God has been teaching him about life in His Kingdom. He now understands that God's purpose through all of those many lessons was to equip him to proclaim those experiences and lessons to the next generation, "So even to old age and gray hairs, O God, do not forsake me, until I proclaim your might to another generation, your power to all those to come" (71:18). In the Kingdom of God, every tight place we experience on our spiritual journey, along with every experience of God's deliverance, is a story we can tell to the next generation. Even now, as you and I read the accounts of the Psalmists and their experiences of struggle and deliverance, we are receiving the lessons passed down to us from prior generations, causing our own faith to be challenged and strengthened. The greatest threat to biblical faith isn't war, famine, plague or bad politics or social policy. The greatest threat to the continuation of biblical faith is the failure of one generation to proclaim God's acts of faithfulness and deliverance to the next generation coming up behind them.

> In the Kingdom of God, every tight place we experience on our spiritual journey, along with every experience of God's deliverance, is a story we can tell to the next generation.

Teaching Through Many Troubles. The Psalmist is refreshingly honest about his relationship with God and what he has been through during his life, "Your righteousness, O God, reaches the high heavens. You who have done great things, O God, who is like you? You who have made me see many troubles and calamities will revive me again" (71:19-20). The phrase "many troubles" includes our Hebrew word for tight places. The Psalmist's declaration that God has made him see many tight places raises a question. How did God make the Psalmist see many tight places? And why? The answer is one that Job could appreciate: By allowing in His wisdom what He could easily have prevented by His power, just as God did with Job. Why? Because there are lessons the Psalmist, along with you and me and generations of believers, could not learn any other way. God is a teacher in His wisdom, and a deliverer in His power, continually working to mold and shape us for life in His Kingdom.

> God is a teacher in His wisdom, and a deliverer in His power, continually working to mold and shape us for life in His Kingdom.

Praising God For His Faithfulness (71:22-24)

It's time for the Psalmist to conclude his song, and he chooses to conclude it with praise for God's faithfulness in all that God has done for him:

"I will also praise you with the harp for your faithfulness, O my God; I will sing praises to you with the lyre, O Holy One of Israel. My lips will shout for joy, when I sing praises to you; my soul also, which you have redeemed. And my tongue will talk of your righteous help all the day long, for they have been put to shame and disappointed who sought to do me hurt" (71:22-24).

And generations of believers, from his generation to ours, continue to learn and grow from the lessons he continues to pass along.

O Lord, our God, we worship You this day with thanksgiving for being the God of all our tight places, and the God of our journey from our youth to our old age. We thank You and bless You, Lord, for the many Kingdom truths You have taught us as we have come to You continually to be our safe refuge and our fortress of protection. In our tight places, You have taught us lessons we could not have learned any other way, as You turned the chaos of our life into the cosmos of Your Kingdom order. Empower us by Your Spirit, O Lord, to faithfully teach the next generation everything You have taught us about Your Kingdom and Your acts of faithfulness in our lives. In the Name of Jesus, and for your glory we ask it. Amen.

Reflections On "Day 23 - Psalm 71 - From Youth To Old Age"
Take few minutes to reflect on what you've discovered through today's devotional.

Insights You Discovered To Reflect On

✍️

✍️

✍️

Raising Your Ebenezer
An Ebenezer is an insight, a principle, or a life lesson that reminds us of what God has done - or is doing - for us on our journey through our tight places. What Ebenezer did you discover for yourself in today's devotional? Use this space to write it out here:

Notes

My Thoughts, Insights, And Reflections

_____
_____
_____
_____
_____
_____
_____
_____

Day 24
Psalm 74
When Everything Crashes And Burns

"O God, why do you cast us off forever?
Why does your anger smoke against the sheep of your pasture?"
(Psalm 74:4)

In the two-dozen Psalm devotionals we have explored up to this point, the emphasis has been almost exclusively on how God works to deliver believers from our personal tight places, along with the lessons He wants to teach us about our spiritual and practical life in His Kingdom. But today's Psalm takes us to a very different place. The Psalmist is about to take us on a journey of asking hard questions in the midst of incredibly challenging circumstances, when a national calamity creates individual tight places. What do we do, what do we believe, and how do we respond when everything we have counted on crashes and burns?

The tight places of life can come in many different forms, including national calamities and their ripple effects. Most of us will never experience the kind of national calamity this Psalm describes, and for that we can be thankful. But other personal calamities can force us into a tight place that challenges both our faith and our hope to the breaking point. The world around us may not be crashing and burning, but our personal world is falling apart, and we are left feeling like everything we have counted on as solid has suddenly turned to sand in a flood. A catastrophic health issue for ourself, a spouse, or a child. The unexpected collapse of a marriage that we thought was secure. A job loss, business failure, or medical bills that cause us to "crash and burn" financially. The world itself may not be crashing and burning, but our personal world certainly is. And we are forced to confront some challenging questions: What do we do, what do we believe, and how do we respond when everything we have counted on crashes and burns?

> What do we do, what do we believe, and how do we respond when everything we have counted on crashes and burns?

When It Feels Like God Has Thrown Us Away (74:1-3)

Why, O God? Before introducing us to the circumstances that inspired such a painful song, the Psalmist offers up a question and a cry, "O God, why do you cast us off forever? Why does your anger smoke against the sheep of your pasture?" It takes little effort to paraphrase the Psalmist's question differently, "O God, why have You thrown us away?" No, God doesn't throw His people away (in case you were wondering), but there are moments when we may feel that way, especially when our personal world is turned upside down and everything we have counted on as reliable seems to be dissolving beneath our feet. If you've never been there, be thankful. If you are there, be encouraged. God isn't done with you yet.

Remember. To feel like God has thrown you away is to feel like you and your problems don't matter to Him, like God has forgotten you. It's one of those life-moments when His silence is deafening. And that's how the Psalmist feels. Forgotten in the Divine silence. And so, from the depths of his pain, he asks God to remember, "Remember your congregation, which you have purchased of old, which you have redeemed to be the tribe of your heritage! Remember Mount Zion, where you have dwelt. Direct your steps to the perpetual ruins; the enemy has destroyed everything in the sanctuary!" (74:2-3)

As we have noted in previous Psalms (see Day 9, Psalm 20 and Day 18, Psalm 44), remembering is an important spiritual concept in the Psalms. It occurs twenty-nine times; fifteen times of men remembering God and His work in their lives, and fourteen times of God remembering His people. Today, a struggling Psalmist calls on God to remember His people in the midst of their tight place. When you and I are in the midst of our tight place, it's as important for us to remember God's past dealings in our lives as it is for God to remember us and what we're going through. He's been there for us before, and He will be there for us now in whatever we're going through. Whether or not we believe and are willing to trust Him, even through darkness and silence, is the difference between faith and fear, the difference between remembering and forgetting.

> Whether or not we believe and are willing to trust Him, even through darkness and silence, is the difference between faith and fear, the difference between remembering and forgetting.

Roars, Signs, And Silence (74:4-11)

At this point, some quick context is in order. What the Psalmist is describing in his song is the Babylonian conquest of Jerusalem by Nebuchadnezzar II, King of Babylon, in 586 B.C. He conquered the city, tore down its walls, looted and burned the temple, and carried thousands of the city's residents off to Babylon as captives and hostages. For God's people on this day, everything *literally* crashed and burned.

Foes Who Roar. In his song, the Psalmist describes how a foreign army has entered and plundered Jerusalem and the temple, "Your foes have roared in the midst of your meeting place; they set up their own signs for signs. They were like those who swing axes in a forest of trees. And all its carved wood they broke down with hatchets and hammers. They set your sanctuary on fire; they profaned the dwelling place of your name, bringing it down to the ground" (74:4-7). Mirroring the language of Isaiah, the Psalmist describes these "foes," people forcing Israel into a tight place, as roaring like a lion (see Isaiah 5:29).

Again, most of us will never face an army of people roaring, slashing, and burning their way through our town or homes (although there are places in our world where this is the literal experience of professing Christians). Our battles may be more quiet, much more personal, and at a deeper spiritual level. In addition to our circumstances and our "people problems," we may find ourselves facing a very real but intangible "foe" who roars like a lion into our thoughts, spreading fear, doubt, and anxiety over whether or not God sees us, hears us, or even cares about what we're going through, "Your adversary the devil prowls around like a roaring lion, seeking someone to devour" (1 Peter 5:8). While our struggle may involve very tangible problems in a very tangible tight place, the spiritual reality remains. We are also struggling with the Adversary of our soul. "We do not wrestle against flesh and blood, but against the rulers, against the authorities, against the cosmic powers over this present darkness, against the spiritual forces of evil in the heavenly places" (Ephesians 6:12). As disciples of the Kingdom, our calling is to recognize the nature of the struggle we are in, and to "Resist him, firm in your faith, knowing that the same kinds of suffering are being experienced by your brotherhood throughout the world" (1 Peter 5:9).

No Signs, No Prophets, No Knowledge. In the midst of his distress, the Psalmist sings and bemoans God's silence, "We do not see our signs; there is no longer any prophet, and there is none among us who knows how long" (74:9).

Most of the 80 occurrences of the Hebrew word "signs" (*'oth*) refer to God's miraculous signs, although it occasionally refers to banners or standards representing individual tribes, as in 74:4.* The Psalmist bemoans that God has gone silent and is no longer speaking to His people, either through His miraculous signs or through His prophets, leaving them to wonder, "How long, O God?" - a question all struggling believers ask at one time or another (see Day 8, Psalm 13 for more on "How long?"). Welcome to what it means to be human, to be a disciple of the Kingdom, and to walk by faith and not by sight (2 Corinthians 5:7). God seldom answers this question directly, choosing instead to simply whisper, "Trust me."

Remembering That God Is King (74:12-17)

Let's be real. Sometimes, in the depths of our struggle, when God is silent and our personal world is crumbling beyond our ability to save it, we have a hard time seeing the Kingdom of God at work in our lives. The Psalmist understands, and in the darkness of God's silence the Psalmist chooses to remember what he has always believed, that whatever happens, God remains King over all, "Yet God my King is from of old, working salvation in the midst of the earth"(74:12). The Psalmist reflects on God's sovereign creative power as King to set the boundaries of His world, and of those who live in it, "You divided the sea by your might; you broke the heads of the sea monsters on the waters . . . Yours is the day, yours also the night; you have established the heavenly lights and the sun. You have fixed all the boundaries of the earth; you have made summer and winter" (74:13-17). When our personal world seems to be falling apart, God is still King, and as King He is "working salvation in the midst of the earth" on our behalf. He may be silent and unseen, but in our darkest moments He remains "the stability of your times, abundance of salvation, wisdom, and knowledge; the fear of the LORD is Zion's treasure" (Isaiah 33:6). Our calling is to remember, and to trust Him, even when we can't see what He is doing.

Arise And Remember! (74:18-23)

As he brings his song to a conclusion, the Psalmist returns to a familiar theme, calling on God to "remember" and to "not forget" three things. *First*, he calls on God to remember those people who have caused this problem and forced God's people into this tight place, saying, "Remember this, O LORD, how the enemy scoffs, and a foolish people reviles your name" (74:18), and again, "Do not forget the clamor of your foes, the uproar of those who rise against you, which goes up continually!" (74:23). *Second*, the Psalmist calls on God to remember the downtrodden, the poor, and the needy, "Let not the downtrodden turn back in shame; let the poor and needy praise your name" (74:21). *Third*, he calls on God to remember the Covenant with His people, and to "defend your cause" (74:20 & 22).

Day 24 - When Everything Crashes And Burns

In the Kingdom of God, remembering is a two-sided coin, a two way street. On one side, God remembers us in the midst of whatever tight place we are experiencing. He remembers how and why it started, and everyone who was involved in creating it. He remembers our faithfulness, the good plans

> In the Kingdom of God, remembering is a two sided coin, a two way street.

He has for us, and the lessons we need to learn to make those plans a reality and a blessing. On the other side, He calls us to remember His past miraculous deeds and faithfulness on our behalf. He hasn't changed. The question is, have we changed and grown?

O Lord, our God, we worship You this day as the God Who is faithful, even in the chaos of our tight place this day. Remember us, O Lord, as we remember all Your past deeds on our behalf, and as we trust You, even in your silence. Father, turn the chaos of our tight place into the cosmos and shalom of Your Kingdom order. This we pray and ask in Jesus' Name. Amen.

Reflections On "Day 24 - Psalm 74 - When Everything Crashes And Burns"
Take few minutes to reflect on what you've discovered through today's devotional.

Insights You Discovered To Reflect On

✍

✍

✍

Raising Your Ebenezer
An Ebenezer is an insight, a principle, or a life lesson that reminds us of what God has done - or is doing - for us on our journey through our tight places. What Ebenezer did you discover for yourself in today's devotional? Use this space to write it out here:

Notes

My Thoughts, Insights, And Reflections

_____
_____
_____
_____
_____
_____
_____
_____

Day 25
Psalm 77
A Deeper Day Of Trouble

"I cry aloud to God, aloud to God, and he will hear me.
In the day of my trouble I seek the Lord;
in the night my hand is stretched out without wearying;
my soul refuses to be comforted."
(Psalm 77:1-2)

The writers, singers, and worship leaders of the Psalms were no strangers to the tight places of life. But in today's devotional, an ancient worship leader and contemporary of David, named Asaph, introduces us to something he refers to as *the day of my trouble* (or, *the day of my tight place*). This isn't a new concept. We saw it earlier in Day 20, Psalm 50. Digging a little deeper we discover that, on five different occasions, both David and Asaph talk about a *day of trouble*, and in another three Psalms the writers refer to *times of trouble*. What today's Psalm reveals is something deeper and more challenging than simply being in a tight place. We've all been there, but this is different, like a tight place on steroids. Today's Psalm reveals a depth of struggle in a day or season of tight places that challenges the faith of the Psalmist to its core and causes him to wonder - maybe even fear - that God Himself has changed.

Has God Changed? (77:1-9)

One of the humanizing characteristics of the Psalms is the honesty of the writers concerning their own struggles with people, circumstances, and with God. And we see those struggles on full display in the first half of today's Psalm. As we read this Psalm, we realize that it's a desperate Psalm penned by a desperate saint who is living through more than just a tight place. He's experiencing what other saints have described as *a dark night of the soul.** He finds no comfort in prayer. The very thought of God causes him to moan and even causes his spirit to faint. He can't sleep, and is so troubled that he can't even put his struggles into words, "When I remember God, I moan; when I meditate, my spirit faints. You hold my eyelids open; I am so troubled that I cannot speak" (77:3-4). Yes, he's in a dark and tight place.

Finally, in the depth of his tight place, Asaph hits rock bottom and asks the

> One of the humanizing characteristics of the Psalms is the honesty of the writers concerning their own struggles with people, circumstances, and with God.

painful questions that struggling saints throughout the ages have wrestled with at one time or another during their own *dark night of the soul*: "Is God done with me? Has His steadfast love toward me come to an end? Are His promises toward me over and done? Has God forgotten me? Is He so angry with me that He will never show me compassion again?" (See 77:8-9). In this dark moment, Asaph genuinely and openly wonders if God has, in fact, forgotten him and no longer cares about the tight place in which he now finds himself. Welcome to Asaph's teachable moment . . . and ours.

In the Kingdom of God, the teachable moments of our life often take place in our darkest moments, those "times of trouble" when our tight places overwhelm us and we find ourselves desperate for answers. But answers without process short-circuit God's teachable moments in our life, like getting answers to math problems without learning

> Answers without process produce believers who are deep in their knowledge but shallow in their faith.

the process needed to find those answers for ourselves. Answers without process produce believers who are deep in their knowledge but shallow in their faith. They live on borrowed answers discovered by people who paid the price to learn them in the days of their own tight places. It's a principle in the Kingdom of God that spiritual maturity is the product of spiritual truth experienced over time. And we seldom embrace life lessons for which we have no genuine experience and have paid little or no price to learn. Teachable moments in the midst of tight places produce life lessons of faith, and long-term spiritual maturity.

A Journey Out And Forward (77:10-19)

Asaph's journey forward out of his tight place began by looking backwards and remembering the years of God's faithfulness and power. "Then I said, 'I will appeal to this, to the years of the right hand of the Most High.' I will remember the deeds of the LORD; yes, I will remember your wonders of old. I will ponder all your work, and meditate on your mighty deeds." (77:10-12)

Asaph's teachable moment began with a choice to remember, to ponder, and to meditate on God's greatness and His mighty deeds of the past, "What god is great like our God? You are the God who works wonders; you have made known your might among the peoples" (77:13-14). Whatever the depth of his tight place might be in his day of his trouble, Asaph realized that God is much deeper and much bigger than his troubles. Perhaps he realized that the God who specializes in acts of miraculous deliverance from impossible situations is able to deliver him, too, just as He delivered "the children of Jacob and Joseph" when He parted the Red Sea. "Your way was through the sea," Asaph declared, "your

Day 25 - A Deeper Day of Trouble

path through the great waters; yet your footprints were unseen" (77:19).

Perhaps the lesson we should learn in the day of our own tight place is to focus our heart's attention not on the size of the problem but on the greatness of God and how He has delivered us in the past. When our journey overwhelms us with troubles and tight places, viewing God's greatness and His

> God's faithfulness to us in the future will mirror His faithfulness to us in our past.

past deliverance in the rear view mirror of our soul is how we discover our true path forward. God's faithfulness to us in the future will mirror His faithfulness to us in our past. Our past tells us where we have been and what He has done for us, and our faith tells us what He can and will do for us in the days ahead. Has God forgotten you? No, He hasn't. The real question is, have we remembered Him, His greatness, and His faithfulness?

Just as He did for Israel at the Red Sea, God is always working for our deliverance during our day of trouble. But as Israel discovered, and as Asaph reminds us, we do not always see His footprints. What Israel saw was a pillar of fire and an open pathway through the sea. And through it all, God was leading them like a Shepherd leading a flock, out of their tight place and into a new and broad place He had already prepared for them. You may not be able to see His footprints today in the midst of your tight place, but He is at work preparing to lead you into a better and broad place. Do you trust Him?

O Lord, our God, we worship You in our day of trouble. Thank You for the lessons of trust You teach us in the day of our tight places. Thank You for the learning process that transforms our knowledge into faith. Lord, empower us to remember all You have done for us in the past, and to trust You for what You are doing for us today, and will do tomorrow. And in those times when we cannot see your footprints, take us by the hand and lead us like a flock, for we are your people, and the sheep of your pasture. For Jesus sake we ask it. Amen.

Reflections On "Day 25 - Psalm 77 - A Deeper Day Of Trouble"
Take few minutes to reflect on what you've discovered through today's devotional.

Insights You Discovered To Reflect On

✍

✍

✍

Raising Your Ebenezer
An Ebenezer is an insight, a principle, or a life lesson that reminds us of what God has done - or is doing - for us on our journey through our tight places. What Ebenezer did you discover for yourself in today's devotional? Use this space to write it out here:

Notes

My Thoughts, Insights, And Reflections

_____

_____

_____

_____

_____

_____

_____

_____

Day 26
Psalm 81
A Tight Place Called Meribah

In distress you called, and I delivered you;
I answered you in the secret place of thunder;
I tested you at the waters of Meribah.
(Psalm 81:7)

The tight places of our life often present us with watershed moments for our walk in the Kingdom of God. Moments when we must choose which side of the watershed we want to live on. Moments of spiritual testing when our responses and choices determine all that follows. Merbiah was one of those watershed moments in the life of God's people. That's the story, and the lesson, of today's Psalm.

Distress, Deliverance, And Testing (81:1-7)

Our Psalm opens with a call to worship and celebrate God's dealings with His people, "Sing aloud to God our strength; shout for joy to the God of Jacob! Raise a song; sound the tambourine, the sweet lyre with the harp. Blow the trumpet at the new moon, at the full moon, on our feast day" (81:1-3).

Psalm 81 is known as a "festal" Psalm, written to celebrate one of Israel's annual festivals or feast days. The particular feast day described here was probably *Sukkot*, or the Feast of Tabernacles (or Booths). That's the annual feast set aside to remember how God provided while Israel lived in temporary dwellings during their forty years of wandering in the Wilderness. In addition to being a time of celebration and worship for all that God had done for them, this was also a time for God's people to remember how God had delivered them, starting with their slavery in Egypt, "I relieved your shoulder of the burden; your hands were freed from the basket" (81:6).

But there was more that God wanted them to remember. "In distress you called, and I delivered you; I answered you in the secret place of thunder; I tested you at the waters of Meribah" (81:7). The word "distress" in verse 7 is our now familiar Hebrew word for tight places. Israel's slavery in Egypt had definitely been one of those tight places. So had their experience at the Red Sea. Both times, the people of Israel called upon God and He miraculously delivered them. But there was another particular tight place that God wanted His people to remember. A tight place called Meribah.

Meribah was the nickname given to two places, and both places were remembered for the same reason: water. The first was located at a spot called Rephidim. Israel camped there less than two months after leaving Egypt (see

Exodus 17:1-7). This place would soon become known as "Massah Meribah." The word "Massah" means "testing" and "Meribah" means "strife." This quickly became a place of testing and strife. At Massah Meribah, the people of Israel complained against God and Moses over God's apparent lack of provision, namely, water. Having witnessed multiple miracles of provision, from parting the Red Sea, to the destruction of the Egyptian army, to His daily provision of food (manna and quail in Exodus 16), God's people now argued with God, and with Moses, over why He hadn't provided water. It got ugly, with the people openly questioning whether or not He could or would provide for them. The episode ended with God commanding Moses to strike a rock with the same rod he had used to part the Red Sea. A later unknown psalmist would describe what happened next, "He opened the rock, and water gushed out; it flowed through the desert like a river" (Psalm 105:41).

This episode at Meribah now became both a tight place and a watershed moment in which God tested the hearts of His people. And such tests are not uncommon. The Hebrew word for test in verse seven (*bachan*) appears nineteen times in the Old Testament (nine times in the Psalms) describing God testing hearts.* In Psalm 66, the Psalmist combines it with the Hebrew word for refining metal to describe God testing and refining His people like precious metal, "For you, O God, have *tested* us; you have *tried* us as silver is *tried*" (Psalm 66:10). In the Kingdom of God, His purpose for our tight places is to reveal the authenticity of our faith and our willingness to trust Him in the midst of challenging circumstances, those circumstances we're calling *tight places*.

God doesn't test us because He's short on information about our hearts or our faith. He tests us because we are easily self-deceived regarding our own spiritual condition. You and I need to discover how authentic our faith is in the practical tight places of life. The self-awareness that comes from such testing is how we learn, grow, and find ourselves able to declare with Job, "But he knows the way that I take; when he has tried me, I shall come out as gold" (Job 23:10). Self-awareness and growth in their willingness to trust Him was God's purpose for His people at that first Meribah, and it continues to be His purpose for His people in our tight places and personal "Meribahs" today.

> God doesn't test us because He's short on information about our hearts or our faith. He tests us because we are easily self-deceived regarding our own spiritual condition.

But thirty-nine years later, Israel found itself facing a second Meribah at a place called Kadesh. We read about it in Numbers 20. Like the Meribah experience of the previous generation, this second Meribah involved the same *tight place*, the same issue - water - and the same quarrel, "Now there was no water for the congregation. And they assembled themselves together against Moses and against Aaron. And the people quarreled with Moses . . ." (Numbers 20:2-3).

Thirty-nine years had passed, and a new generation had risen up, but God's people found themselves in the same tight place, questioning God's provision, and even His ability to provide. In a broader sense, the issue wasn't water. The issue was faith and obedience. Both Meribahs involved a lack of faith in God's plan, purposes, and provision for His people. God's plan was to bring them into the land He had promised to them, to Abraham and to his descendants. His purpose was to build their faith and to teach His people what it means - in very practical terms - to trust and obey.

For thirty-nine years, God had faithfully demonstrated His daily provision with manna and quail. This second Meribah was another watershed moment, a test of their faith, of their obedience, and of what they had learned over those thirty-nine years. Through this test they could discover truths about themselves. But their moment of self-discovery became a moment of unbelief, and one that came at a high price for Moses and Aaron. Just as he had done 39 years earlier, Moses struck the rock, rather than speaking to the rock as God now commanded. Water poured from the rock, just as before. But Moses' act of disobedience and unbelief, publicly dishonored God and prevented both Moses and Aaron from entering the promised land, "And the LORD said to Moses and Aaron, 'Because you did not believe in me, to uphold me as holy in the eyes of the people of Israel, therefore you shall not bring this assembly into the land that I have given them'" (Numbers 20:12). We've arrived at a watershed life lesson on our journey through tight places. How we respond to our tight places, in faith or unbelief, in obedience or disobedience, can have a profound impact, not only on our own spiritual condition, but on the spiritual condition of those around us. Just ask Moses and Aaron.

A Failed Test, A Lesson Not Learned (81:8-16)

Three times in this Psalm, the Psalmist talks about the importance of Israel listening to God, "O Israel, if you would but listen to me!" God declares (81:8). And again, "But my people did not listen to my voice; Israel would not submit to me"(81:11). It's impossible to obey God if we choose not to listen to what He is telling us. It is often in the tight places of our life

> It is often in the tight places of our life that God speaks the loudest, perhaps because that's where we're the most willing to listen.

that God speaks the loudest, perhaps because that's where we're the most willing to listen. In his book, *The Problem of Pain*, C.S. Lewis notes, "God whispers to us in our pleasures, speaks in our conscience, but shouts in our pains: it is his megaphone to rouse a deaf world." The same is true of our tight places. God is speaking to us through them. The question hanging in the air is simple: are we listening to what He has to say? All He may be saying is, *"Trust me. I've got this, and I've got you."*

What He said through the Psalmist was, "Oh, that my people would listen to me, that Israel would walk in my ways! I would soon subdue their enemies and turn my hand against their foes"(81:13-14). Once again, the word *foes* translates our Hebrew word for tight places. He reminds us that listening, believing, trusting, and obeying are the responses God seeks from us. He is more than able to resolve whatever tight place we may be experiencing. But His greater goal in that moment is our spiritual growth, as we learn to hear, to trust, and to obey. Our challenge is to remember that there is a Meribah moment in every tight place we experience. What Meribah moment are you facing today? Which side of this spiritual watershed will the Lord find you on tomorrow because of how you respond today?

> Our challenge is to remember that there is a Meribah moment in every tight place we experience.

O Lord, our God, we worship You today in the midst of our tight place. Thank You for the lessons You teach us in our tight places. Today we meet You at Meribah and declare that You have always provided for us and delivered us. In today's watershed moment, we choose faith over unbelief and fear, and obedience over disobedience. Today we trust You and ask You to provide for us and to deliver us once again. May our choices in our watershed moment this day impact those around us for the Kingdom of God and for Your glory. For Jesus sake we ask it. Amen.

Day 26 - A Tight Place Called Meribah

Reflections On "Day 26 - Psalm 81 - A Tight Place Called Meribah"
Take few minutes to reflect on what you've discovered through today's devotional.

Insights You Discovered To Reflect On

🖎

🖎

🖎

Raising Your Ebenezer
An Ebenezer is an insight, a principle, or a life lesson that reminds us of what God has done - or is doing - for us on our journey through our tight places. What Ebenezer did you discover for yourself in today's devotional? Use this space to write it out here:

Notes

My Thoughts, Insights, And Reflections

_____

_____

_____

_____

_____

_____

_____

_____

Day 27
Psalm 86
Regaining Our Focus

"In the day of my trouble I call upon you,
for you answer me."
(Psalm 86:7)

Today's Psalm is a prayer sung by David about an unknown "day of my trouble." He never tells us the circumstances that produced this prayerful song. What we can gather from David's song suggests that, like many of us, he is lonely, poor and needy, and in trouble (yes, our word for a *tight place*). Who among us hasn't been there and felt that way at one time or another. Maybe you're there today as you read this devotional. Thankfully, David offers us some thoughts on how to respond during our own "day of trouble."

Preserve Us In The Day of Our Trouble (86:1-13)

David never tells us the circumstances behind his tight place. But his prayerful cry for God to hear and answer sounds less like the cry of a king, and more like the cry of a man who has spent years fleeing the wrath of King Saul. Something to consider, although we can't be certain. As David prays for God's help in his "day of trouble" (see 86:7), he offers several reasons why God should act on his behalf . . . and ours.

Poor And Needy. David opens his prayer by describing himself with words of poverty and distress, "Incline your ear, O LORD, and answer me, for I am poor and needy" (86:1). This will be the fourth time that our Psalms of tight places have mentioned the "poor and needy."* The phrase occurs eight times in the

> God is always attentive to the prayers of His people who have fallen on hard times.

Psalms, and sixteen times in the Old Testament. "Poor" (*'ani*) describes someone who is disadvantaged and struggling with some kind of disability or distress, while "needy" (*'ebyon*) describes someone who is poor in a material sense and has fallen on hard times.* The "poor and needy" of the Old Testament are believers who cry out to God for help when there is no one else to help them. God's ear is always attentive to the cry of the "poor and needy" among His people, and He promises to answer them, "When the poor and needy seek water, and there is none, and their tongue is parched with thirst, I the LORD will answer them; I, the God of Israel, will not forsake them" (Isaiah 41:17).*

Maybe you've never considered yourself "poor and needy." If you've never been there, be thankful and consider yourself blessed. But if you find yourself there - distressed and in a financial tight place - be encouraged. God is always attentive to the prayers of His people who have fallen on hard times. He promises, "I, the God of Israel, will not forsake them." And today, that includes you.

Your People And Your Servant. David offers two reasons why God should answer his prayers and act on his behalf, "Preserve my life, for I am *godly*; save your *servant*, who trusts in you—you are my God" (86:2). David begins by declaring, "for I am godly." The word for "godly" (*chasid*) shows up twenty-five times in the Psalms describing God's people as the objects of His steadfast love.* The equivalent New Testament word would be "saints" (*hagios*). The New Testament writers use *hagios* sixty times to describe New Testament believers. David's reason for why God should answer his prayers is simple: "I'm one of your believing people. I belong to you." And what was true of David is also true of every follower and believer in Jesus. We belong to Him, and our prayers and our needs matter to Him. Today, *you* matter to Him.

But David offers a second reason for why God should answer his prayers and act on his behalf, "save your servant, who trusts in you—you are my God." Not only is David one of God's believing people, he has bound himself to God as His servant (*'ebed*). And, yes, there's a New Testament equivalent. When the Old Testament was translated into Greek (the

> As disciples of the Kingdom and followers and believers in Jesus, we are bound to Him, and He is bound to us.

Septuagint), the Hebrew word *'ebed* (*slave, servant*) was translated by the Greek *doulos*, meaning *slave* or *bond-servant*. It occurs more than two-dozen times in the New Testament letters describing followers and believers in Jesus. The Apostle Paul uses it to describe himself and his own relationship with God, "Paul, a *servant* of Christ Jesus, called to be an apostle, set apart for the gospel of God" (Romans 1:1; see Titus 1:1). As disciples of the Kingdom and followers and believers in Jesus, we are bound to Him, and He is bound to us. We are His bond-servants, and our prayers and our needs matter to Him.

Steadfast Love. Three times in today's Psalm, David refers to God's steadfast love, "For you, O Lord, are good and forgiving, *abounding in steadfast love* to all who call upon you" (86:5). God's steadfast love (Hebrew *chesed*) is His covenant-keeping love that binds Him to us for our good. Eight times in the Old Testament, including two in today's Psalm, God's steadfast love is described as "great" or "abounding."* God's covenant-keeping love is measureless, and His measureless love "abounds" toward His people. He is bound to us for our good and doesn't give up on us when we're struggling in our tight places. People may give up and walk away from us, but God never does, and never will.

Day 27 - Regaining Our Focus

Regaining Our Focus. When you and I are struggling through our personal tight place, it's easy to become overwhelmed by it all and to lose our focus, especially when God is working *quietly* behind the scene for our deliverance. David understood. And to regain his focus, David chooses to sing and glorify God's name (vs 9), to sing about the *wondrous things* God has done (vs 10), to sing about His great *steadfast love* (vs 5, 13), to sing about being one of His *"godly" people* and His *bond-servant* (vs 2), all the while giving thanks with his whole heart (vs 12). David's song of praise gives us an example of how you and I can choose to regain our focus when we find ourselves "between a rock and a hard place" in our own day of trouble. The choice is ours. What will you choose today?

A Sign Of Your Favor (86:14-17)

It's time for David to conclude his song. True to his choice to focus on God's greatness, David boldly appropriates and sings the words of God's self-revelation to Moses in Exodus 34:6, "But you, O Lord, are a God merciful and gracious, slow to anger and abounding in steadfast love and faithfulness" (86:15). Standing on his declaration of God being "merciful and gracious," David calls on God to "turn to me and be gracious to me; give your strength to your servant, and save the son of your maidservant" (86:16). David concludes his song with a request that has a familiar ring to it, something multitudes of struggling saints have asked for, if only in the silence of their own hearts, "Show me a sign of your favor, that those who hate me may see and be put to shame because you, LORD, have helped me and comforted me" (86:17).

Like so many of us struggling through life's tight places, David yearns for God's vindication of his journey, some outward and tangible sign of God's goodness toward His people who are called by His name, the God on whom all of us have set our hope. Today, let's turn our hope and our yearning into our prayers and songs of praise.

O Lord, our God, we worship You this day in the midst of our tight place. Poor and needy, we come to You as Your people. You and You alone are our God, and we are Your servants. Thank You for being attentive to our prayers and for making us the objects of Your steadfast love. We confess that there are times when we are overwhelmed by everything that's happening in our tight place, and we easily lose our focus. Turn to us and be gracious to us, O Lord. Show us a sign of Your favor and vindicate us, for we are Your people, called by Your Name. And You are our God, on whom we have set our hope. For Jesus sake and in His Name we ask it. Amen.

Reflections On "Day 27 - Psalm 86 - Regaining Our Focus"

Take few minutes to reflect on what you've discovered through today's devotional.

Insights You Discovered To Reflect On

🖎

🖎

🖎

Raising Your Ebenezer

An Ebenezer is an insight, a principle, or a life lesson that reminds us of what God has done - or is doing - for us on our journey through our tight places. What Ebenezer did you discover for yourself in today's devotional? Use this space to write it out here:

Notes

My Thoughts, Insights, And Reflections

_____

_____

_____

_____

_____

_____

_____

_____

Day 28
Psalm 91
In The Shadow Of The Almighty

"He who dwells in the shelter of the Most High
will abide in the shadow of the Almighty."
(Psalm 91:11)

Today's Psalm is a song for dangerous times. A common theme among God's worshiping people. But it is also a song about God's miraculous protection of His people when they have no choice but to obey and to walk through dangerous tight places. The Psalm is anonymous. We don't know who wrote it, or what they were experiencing that caused them to sing about such danger and deliverance. It frequently sounds like David, which is probably why the translators of the Old Testament from Hebrew into Greek (the *Septuagint*) credited David as the author. But embracing the message of the song is more important than figuring out who wrote it or why. It's a song about all of God's people, including you and me, and the protection we enjoy when we choose to take refuge "in the shadow of the Almighty."

A Four-Fold Protection (91:1-2)

As he opens his song, our unknown Psalmist uses four of God's names to highlight the protection enjoyed by the believer, "He who dwells in the shelter of the *Most High* (*'elyon*) will abide in the shadow of the *Almighty* (*shaddai*). I will say to the LORD (YHWH), 'My refuge and my fortress, my *God* (*'elohim*), in whom I trust." The Psalmist's point is clear. As believers, we enjoy the protection of God's complete nature and power. Everything He is as God protects us from everything we might face as His people. There is no greater protection than to be surrounded by God in His fullness.

> Everything He is as God protects us from everything we might face as His people.

God's Diverse Protection (91:3-13)

A Shield And Buckler. God's complete protection, and the deliverance He gives each of us, are as diverse as His people and the tight places they face. To make his point, the Psalmist uses a variety of illustrations and metaphors, "For he will deliver you from *the snare of the fowler* and from *the deadly pestilence*. He will cover you with his pinions, and under his wings you will find refuge; his faithfulness is a *shield and buckler*" (91:3-4). A little background might be helpful here. In ancient times, warriors often employed two types of shields. They used a large shield for protection during an attack from arrows or spears. They also used a smaller shield called a *buckler*, worn on the wrist or forearm, when combat became hand-to-hand. It can be a challenge for present-day believers to relate to such battles, dangers, and metaphors. But the Psalmist's point is simple and enduring over the centuries. In the tight places of our life, God's faithfulness toward us is a large shield of protection when we are under attack, and a

> Whatever threatening tight place you and I may be facing, God's faithfulness protects us like a warrior with "shield and buckler."

small shield when we feel like we're in hand-to-hand combat with circumstances, people, and the Enemy of our soul. Whatever threatening tight place you and I may be facing today, God's faithfulness protects us like a warrior with "shield and buckler." And He cares for us, protecting us personally like a mother bird protects her chicks.

When The Battle Gets Personal. There are times when our struggle in tight places becomes very personal. In the space of four verses the personal pronouns "you" or "your" occur nine times as the Psalmist turns his song directly to his listeners and sings about God's protection toward them when the battle gets personal. "A thousand may fall at *your* side, ten thousand at *your* right hand, but it will not come near *you*. *You* will only look with *your* eyes and see the recompense of the wicked. Because *you* have made the LORD *your* dwelling place— the Most High, who is my refuge— no evil shall be allowed to befall *you*, no plague come near *your* tent" (91:7-10). Few

> When the struggle in our tight place gets personal, so does God's protection.

of us will ever find ourselves in a situation where a thousand or ten thousand people are falling beside us. The Psalmist uses hyperbole to describe a personal situation that is potentially dangerous and is definitely overwhelming. He wants us to know that when the struggle in our tight place gets personal, so does God's protection.

In the Kingdom of God, the promises of protection for those who take refuge in Him are broad and encompassing, but they are also carefully fashioned according to God's Kingdom will and purpose for each individual believer. We see this in the New Testament when Paul writes, "And we know that for those who love God all things work together for good, for those who are called according to his purpose" (Romans 8:28). Seven verses later the Apostle explains more about God's purposes and protection, "Who shall separate us from the love of Christ? Shall tribulation, or distress, or persecution, or famine, or nakedness, or danger, or sword? As it is written, 'For your sake we are being killed all the day long; we are regarded as sheep to be slaughtered.' No, in all these things we are more than conquerors through him who loved us" (Romans 8:35-37).

On January 8, 1956, five Christian missionaries (Jim Elliot, Nate Saint, Ed McCully, Peter Flemming, and Roger Youderian) died at the hands of the Huaorani Indians of Ecuador. The five men were attempting to make direct contact with the tribe in the hope of sharing the gospel of Jesus Christ with the reclusive tribe. In a book she wrote two years after his death, Jim Elliot's widow, Elizabeth Elliot, told the story of what took place. She titled the book *In The Shadow of The Almighty*.

God's protection doesn't mean we won't experience tribulation, or distress, or persecution, or famine, or nakedness, or danger, or sword. And anyone who teaches otherwise denies the clear teaching of Scripture. God's protection doesn't keep us from difficult or dangerous times. It keeps us through them. As Pastor John Piper observed in an article about

> God's protection doesn't keep us from difficult or dangerous times. It keeps us through them.

that 1956 event, "the refuge of the people of God is not a refuge from suffering and death, but a refuge from final and ultimate defeat."* God's protection and purpose for each of us today means there is no person, circumstance, or tight place we can experience that can separate us from the love of God in Christ Jesus. Whatever you and I are going through today, our calling as disciples of His Kingdom is to take refuge in Him, to abide in the shadow of the Almighty, and to trust Him to be our shield and buckler.

Even The Angels Get Involved. But the Psalmist isn't quite done singing about the extent of God's protection. He turns his song to the role of the angelic host in our protection and deliverance. "For he will command his angels concerning you to guard you in all your ways. On their hands they will bear you up, lest you strike your foot against a stone" (91:11-12). One of the most frequent (and important) names of God in the Old Testament is "the LORD of hosts" (*Jehovah-Sabbaoth*), appearing over 240 times. He is "the God of heaven's armies." From Genesis to Revelation, angels make frequent appearances, carrying out God's purposes and serving God's people. A quick word study reveals angels being mentioned some two hundred times. Sometimes as God's messengers. Sometimes delivering God's people. Announcing the birth of Jesus. Engineering a jail break for Peter. Encouraging the Apostle Paul. Carrying out God's end-time plans. When it comes to angelic intervention and protection during the season of our tight places, you and I will never know (at least on this side of eternity) how many times God's angelic host have intervened on our behalf and have stood between us and disaster.

Eight Promises We Can Trust (91:14-16)

"Because he holds fast to me in love, I will deliver him; I will protect him, because he knows my name. When he calls to me, I will answer him; I will be with him in trouble; I will rescue him and honor him. With long life I will satisfy him and show him my salvation." (91:14-15)

The Psalmist is approaching the end of his song. And as if to summarize the day's lessons, the Psalmist shares eight promises directly from God to all who choose to call upon Him, to trust Him, and to take refuge in Him: "Because he holds fast to me in love, I will *deliver him*; I will *protect him*, because he knows my name. When he calls to me, I will *answer him*; I will *be with him* in trouble; I will *rescue him* and *honor him*. With long life I will *satisfy him* and *show him my salvation*." In the Kingdom of God, you and I are not spared trouble - the tight places of life. But in God's Kingdom plan and purpose for our life, our tight places become the seasons when our faith is tested and refined as God demonstrates His steadfast love and His faithfulness to all the promises He has made to us, and to all who choose to dwell "in the Shadow of the Almighty."

O Lord, our God, we thank You and bless You this day for Your many and diverse protections in the day of our tight place. Thank You that everything You are as God rises up to surround and protect us from everything we are facing in our tight place today. You are our shield and buckler, protecting us in battles large and small, and even the ones that are deeply personal. Thank You for unseen angelic protection, and the troubles You have saved us from that we never even knew about. We worship You in this season as You refine and test our faith. Father, empower us today to embrace Your faithfulness to fulfill all the promises you have made to us who daily choose to dwell in the shadow of the Almighty. In Jesus' Name and for Your glory we pray. Amen.

Reflections On "Day 28 - Psalm 91 - Protection Under His Wings"
Take few minutes to reflect on what you've discovered through today's devotional.

Insights You Discovered To Reflect On

✍

✍

✍

Raising Your Ebenezer
An Ebenezer is an insight, a principle, or a life lesson that reminds us of what God has done - or is doing - for us on our journey through our tight places. What Ebenezer did you discover for yourself in today's devotional? Use this space to write it out here:

Notes

My Thoughts, Insights, And Reflections

_____

_____

_____

_____

_____

_____

_____

_____

_____

Day 29
Psalm 102
When God Hides Himself

"Hear my prayer, O LORD; let my cry come to you!
Do not hide your face from me in the day of my distress!
Incline your ear to me;
answer me speedily in the day when I call!"
(Psalm 102:1-2)

As we've already discovered on our journey through the Psalms of tight places, there are times in the life of the Psalmists, and perhaps in the life of every believer, when God feels distant, when His Presence is hard to find, when it feels like our prayers are bouncing off a brass ceiling, and when God's silence is deafening. We've heard the Psalmist bemoan God's silent and distant times (Day 24, Psalm 74). As you read this, you may have experienced such a time (or times) when, in the darkness of His silence, you have wondered, "Has God hidden Himself from me?" This Psalm is about one of those times in the life of the Psalmist.

An Introduction That Tells It All (102:1a)

The introduction to this Psalm sums up the situation with a single sentence, *"A Prayer of the afflicted, when he is faint, and pours out his complaint before the Lord."* This is the description of a struggling saint. So we can better understand his struggle, we're going to unpack this introduction by looking at three Hebrew words.

Afflicted. As we discovered earlier, the word *afflicted* (*'ani*)* is one of the primary Hebrew words for the poor, someone who is economically disadvantaged, socially distressed, and possibly disabled. *Afflicted* is a summary description of a saint who is hurting.

Faint. The word *faint* (*'ataph*)* describes someone who looks at their situation, sees themselves separated from God, and feels emotionally and physically exhausted and overwhelmed. Jonah uses this word to describe himself in the belly of the great fish, "When my life was *fainting* away, I remembered the LORD, and my prayer came to you, into your holy temple" (Jonah 2:7). I'm fairly certain that the belly of a great fish qualifies as a tight place. And in that tight place, Jonah was emotionally overwhelmed and exhausted. And so is our Psalmist.

Complaint. The word *complaint* (*sinach*)* describes a thought or meditation. In a context like this, it describes a complaint. Sometimes, the longer we meditate on our situation, the worse it seems, and our thoughts soon become a complaint before the Lord. This Psalm is a prayer expressing the thoughts and emotions of a struggling saint who, like Jonah, finds himself in what feels like an impossible situation, exhausted and overwhelmed, with no strength to fight it. Yes, he's in a *tight place*. If you've never been there, give thanks. If you are there, be encouraged. There's more to the story.

The Day Of My Distress (102:1b-11)

The Psalmist describes his tight place as *the day of my distress*, "Hear my prayer, O LORD; let my cry come to you! Do not hide your face from me in *the day of my distress!* Incline your ear to me; answer me speedily in the day when I call!" (102:1b - 2). We saw this idea earlier in Day 25, Psalm 77. The same Hebrew phrase, just a different translation. There, Asaph openly wondered if God had forgotten him. In today's Psalm, an un-named Psalmist openly wonders why God is hiding His face during a tight place so challenging he could compare it with Jonah in the belly of the great fish.

If you and I are honest, we would admit to times when we've wondered where God has gone and why He seems so silent in those times when we need Him the most. Job wondered and pondered the same question, "Why do you hide your face and count me as your enemy?" (Job 13:24). And Job isn't alone. On nine different occasions, Psalmists ask the same question, "How long, O Lord? Will you forget me forever? How long will you hide your face from me?"*

> Wondering where God has gone and why He is hiding His face from us is a shared experience among God's struggling people.

Wondering where God has gone and why He is hiding His face is a shared experience among God's struggling people.

Through nine verses (102:3-11), our Psalmist details his day of distress, the affliction he has experienced, his internal struggles (wasted days, bodily aches, a broken heart, loneliness, and isolation), the reproach of people who see what he is going through, and feeling cursed by men and abandoned by God. He feels as transient as a fading shadow and as withering grass.* And did we mention that the word *feeble* in the introductory verse of this Psalm can also describe someone who's depressed? So, yes, there's probably some of that going on, too. Put all of that together, and it's a pretty tight place and a pretty deep spiritual hole the Psalmist finds himself in.

Let's be real. If you're in a tight place that feels as hopeless as Jonah stuck in the belly of a great fish for three days with no way out, then afflicted, feeble, and depressed is probably a good description (maybe even an understatement). In a moment like this, "Why has God hidden his face from me" feels like an honest and reasonable question to ask. And attributing your suffering to God's displeasure - not to mention the curses of men - probably feels like a plausible answer. Our tight places can twist our feelings in directions we wouldn't otherwise go.

> Our tight places can twist our feelings in directions we wouldn't otherwise go.

The Appointed Time Has Come (102:13-22)

But the story doesn't end here. Suddenly, we discover ourselves at a turning point in the Psalmist's song. He now turns his thoughts from focusing on himself and the challenges of his tight place to focusing on God's compassion, graciousness, pity, and even His greater Kingdom purposes. "Thou wilt arise and have compassion on Zion," he declares, "For it is time to be gracious to her, For the appointed time has come" (102:13).

We've arrived at an important teachable moment in the tight place of our Psalmist as he embraces a reality that we all need to embrace during our own day of distress. God has purposes and appointed times for the work He is doing in our lives. His ultimate Kingdom purpose for the Psalmist, and for each of us, is that "Nations will fear the name of the LORD, and all the kings of the earth will fear your glory" (102:15). God's glory among "the nations and all the kings of the earth" starts by glorifying Himself through the lessons He teaches each of us in our tight places during our personal "day of distress." For each of us, glorifying God begins when we see our tight place through the lens of the Kingdom of God, seeing it as His tool for our discipleship in His Kingdom.

> For each of us, glorifying God begins by seeing our tight place through the lens of the Kingdom of God and our place in it.

No longer focused on himself and his tight place, the Psalmist focuses on another truth - God does not ignore our prayers of destitution. We may be financially distressed, socially excluded, physically, mentally, emotionally, and spiritually exhausted and overwhelmed by what we are going through, but God hears our prayers, "He regards the prayer of the destitute, and has not despised their prayer" (102:17). God hears you, and He isn't done yet.

His Years And Our Years (102:23-28)

A silver thread runs through this Psalm, tying the several parts together. It's the thread of our transience and God's eternity. Simply stated, our lives are short, like smoke that quickly vanishes, or like grass that quickly withers. This silver thread reminds us that we are all in a race against time, a race to fulfill God's Kingdom purposes before our health fails, before our wealth fails, and before life itself fails. And so the Psalmist declares, "'O my God,' I say, take me not away in the midst of my days - you whose years endure throughout all generations!" (102:24). In spite of the shortness of our lives, the good news is that God wants to do something in and through us and our tight places that will create *Kingdom ripple effects* and impact future generations,

> In spite of the shortness of our lives, the good news is that God wants to do something in and through us and our tight places that will create "Kingdom ripple effects" and impact future generations.

"Let this be recorded for a generation to come, so that a people yet to be created may praise the LORD" (102:18).

So, does God hide His face from us in the day of our tight places? No, He doesn't, although it may feel like it. As David declares in a different Psalm, "You who fear the LORD, praise him! All you offspring of Jacob, glorify him, and stand in awe of him, all you offspring of Israel! For he has not despised or abhorred the affliction of the afflicted, and he has not hidden his face from him, but has heard, when he cried to him" (Psalm 22:23-24).

No, God has not hidden Himself from you, regardless of how you may feel today. Make this the day you see your tight place through the lens of the Kingdom of God, the day you focus on God's Kingdom purposes for your life, and on the *Kingdom ripple effects* He wants to create, and the impact He wants you to have on generations to come. God's Kingdom vision for you is bigger than your Kingdom vision for yourself, and He isn't done with you yet.

O Lord, our God, we worship You today, thankful that You do not hide your face from us in the days of our distress, but You hear and answer our desperate prayers. Eternal Father, remember the shortness of our lives and our race against time. Work through us, O God, and empower us to accomplish Kingdom purposes that will impact generations yet to come, that a people yet to be created may praise the Lord and glorify Your great Name. For Jesus sake we ask it. Amen.

Reflections On "Day 29 - Psalm 102 - When God Hides Himself"
Take few minutes to reflect on what you've discovered through today's devotional.

Insights You Discovered To Reflect On

🖎

🖎

🖎

Raising Your Ebenezer
An Ebenezer is an insight, a principle, or a life lesson that reminds us of what God has done - or is doing - for us on our journey through our tight places. What Ebenezer did you discover for yourself in today's devotional? Use this space to write it out here:

Notes

My Thoughts, Insights, And Reflections

_____
_____
_____
_____
_____
_____
_____
_____
_____

Day 30
Psalm 107
Thanksgiving For Steadfast Love

"Oh give thanks to the LORD, for he is good,
for his steadfast love endures forever!
Let the redeemed of the LORD say so,
whom he has redeemed from trouble."
(Psalm 107:1-2)

If you and I were to go looking for one Psalm to sum up what the Psalms teach us about God's dealings with His people during the season of their tight places, we would quickly find it in Psalm 107.

A Better Tone and a Better Focus (107:1-3)

"Oh give thanks to the LORD, for he is good, for his steadfast love endures forever! Let the redeemed of the LORD say so, whom he has redeemed from trouble and gathered in from the lands, from the east and from the west, from the north and from the south" (107:1-3)

Starting in these opening verses, the tone and focus of the Psalmist turns to thankfulness for God's steadfast love that redeems us from our tight places. Our Hebrew word for tight places occurs five times in this Psalm, translated as "trouble." And the refrain, "Let them thank the LORD for his steadfast love, for his wondrous works to the children of man!" occurs four times as well. The Psalmist connects his thanksgiving with God's steadfast love, and then connects God's steadfast love with His work of delivering His people from their tight places. He calls on everyone who has been delivered to speak out, giving thanks for God's steadfast love, for hearing their heart-felt cries, and for delivering them when all realistic hope of deliverance had been lost.

Curiously, verse two of this Psalm gets frequently quoted, but usually out of context. "Let the redeemed of the LORD say so," is what we like to proclaim, usually referring to testimonies of individual salvation experiences. While such testimonies are certainly a good thing, what the Psalmist actually urges here is for believers who have been delivered from their seemingly impossible *tight places* to speak out and glorify God by giving thanks for His steadfast love and for their deliverance.

On reflection, the larger focus of today's Psalm isn't so much on our *tight places* as it is on God's *steadfast love*. Five times in this Psalm the writer pairs *tight places*, and our deliverance from them, with God's *steadfast love*, an attribute of His character and His primary motivation for everything He does to deliver us. The Hebrew word for steadfast love (*chesed*) can be variously understood as kindness, love, steadfast love, lovingkindness, and mercy.* God's *chesed* isn't an emotional attachment to people or things. There's a different Hebrew word for that kind of love.* God's steadfast love is His covenant-keeping love that binds Him to His people for their good. God's steadfast, covenant-keeping love means He doesn't give up on us, regardless of

> God's steadfast, covenant-keeping love means He doesn't give up on us, regardless of our tight places.

our tight places (and the Psalmist will soon give us four examples). Today's Psalm connects God's *chesed* with our *tight places*, making it clear that our struggles are not a sign that God doesn't love or care about us. No, just the opposite! The Psalmist wants us to see God's deliverance as the tangible, practical expression of His steadfast, unwavering, covenant-keeping mercy, love, and concern toward all who trust Him in the midst of their tight place.

Deliverance From A Variety of Tight Places (107:4-32)

To illustrate God's steadfast love toward believers in tight places, the Psalmist uses four different groups of people and their struggles in four very different tight places. Homeless wanderers. Rebellious prisoners. Foolish sinners. Storm-tossed sailors. These groups illustrate diversity. They aren't exclusive ("only these groups and no more"). More about them in a moment.

If we could discern the writer's thinking, we might discover that his goal is to encourage every worshiping believer, regardless of their tight place and how they got there, that God's steadfast love doesn't change based on their circumstances. God is attentive to their cries, and He is already quietly at work for their deliverance. The Psalmist wants us to find hope in the examples of others.

The beauty and strength of this Psalm is found in the diversity of people and the consistency of God's dealings. While each people-group is unique, each group is treated in the same five steps:

1) Who they are and what they've done,

2) How they cried out to God in the midst of their tight place (*Then they cried to the LORD in their trouble, and he delivered them from their distress*),

3) How God resolved their tight place,

4) How they should respond (*Let them thank the LORD for his steadfast love, for his wondrous works to the children of man!*) and,

5) A conclusion unique to that group.

This structure repeats itself four times through four groups. Why? Perhaps because the Psalmist wants us to understand that, in His steadfast love, God is consistent, and treats His people equally, even when He treats them differently

Day 30 - Thanksgiving For Steadfast Love

and uniquely. God's will for each of us, and His response to our individual tight places, isn't a cookie-cutter pattern or a formula. It's personal. He knows us and understands us, better than we know or understand ourselves. And each group below is in their own unique tight place.

Homeless Wanderers (107:4-9) - My wife and I have worked among the homeless and marginalized of our community for some 25 years. Long story. I've pastored them, counseled them, married them, buried them and for ten months I helped manage the largest homeless camp in the State of Washington with over 689 residents.* One of the enduring lessons from our journey through those years is that there are

> God's will for each of us, and His response to our individual tight places, isn't a cookie-cutter pattern or a formula. It's personal.

no such things as "homeless people." There are only people who, for a season of their life, and for many different reasons, are experiencing what it means to be "homeless wanderers," people who have no city - or home - of their own. For the homeless wanderers, God "led them by a straight way till they reached a city to dwell in" (107:7).

Rebellious Prisoners (107:10-16) - People find themselves prisoners "in affliction and in irons" for a wide variety of reasons. The reason given by the Psalmist is "they had rebelled against the words of God, and spurned the counsel of the Most High" (107:11). Some prisons and irons are very literal. Others are metaphorical, but still very real. Some people are prisoners to spiritual "darkness and the shadow of death" and to their unbelief, some to the consequences of disobedience (as the Psalmist suggests here), some to broken relationships, some to financial bondage. The prophet Isaiah refers more generally to bonds of wickedness and yokes of oppression (Isaiah 58:6). The good news for prisoners of all reasons and of all descriptions is that the Kingdom of God "shatters the doors of bronze and cuts in two the bars of iron" (107:16), and delivers them from "darkness and the shadow of death" (See Day 10, Psalm 23).

Foolish Sinners (107:17-22) - Someone once observed that, according to the book of Proverbs, a fool is someone who acts without regard to consequences. It's an observation that seems uniquely appropriate for *Foolish Sinners*, individuals who sin without regard to consequences, and who "because of their iniquities suffered affliction" (107:17). Yes, we all reap the consequences of the foolishness we have sown. The good news is that God, in His mercy and steadfast love, "sent out his word and healed them, and delivered them from their destruction" (107:20).

Storm-Tossed Sailors (107:23-32) - There's a lesson here bigger than Israel, ships, or sailors. It's about our life in this world. We live in this created order by permission and, as experienced by storm-tossed sailors, it is frequently out of our control. In the midst of our tight places, it can bring us to a point where we too are "at (our) wits' end" (107:27). The good news is that, like Jesus and His disciples in a storm on the Sea of Galilee (Matthew 8:23-27), God is able to still the storms of our tight places and bring us safely through, "He made the storm be still, and the waves of the sea were hushed . . . and he brought them to their desired haven" (107:29-30).

Celebrating God's Awesome Deeds of Deliverance (107:33-43)

Through the ever changing situations of very different people and a wide variety of tight places - "troubles" - God's steadfast love for His people, His attentiveness to their cries, and His willingness to deliver, do not change. And repetition is the Psalmist's way of driving this point home to struggling believers who can be slow to understand. God really does cause all things - including our tight places - to work together for our good (Romans 8:28) as he unfolds our deliverance. Through repetition, the Psalmist wants us to find hope in these examples of God's consistency, faithfulness, and steadfast love toward all who trust Him in the midst of their tight places.

So, whoever you may be, whatever you may have done, whatever tight place you may find yourself in, and regardless of how you got there, God's love and concern for you is steadfast and unchanging. He hears your heartfelt prayers. He is quietly at work - even now - for your deliverance. His only requirements on your part are your need, your faith, and your repentance. Everything else will come in time.

O Lord, our God, we worship You today with thanksgiving for your steadfast love that seeks us, finds us, and delivers us from our tight places. Thank You for hearing our heartfelt cries as wanderers without a home, prisoners in chains, fools in our sin, and people who have given up hope at our wits end in the storm of our life. Use our struggle, our story of deliverance, and our praise, O God, to accomplish your Kingdom purposes, to glorify Your great Name, and to encourage others to trust You for deliverance from their tight places. For Your glory and for Jesus sake we ask it. Amen.

Reflections On "Day 30 - Psalm 107 - Thanksgiving For Steadfast Love"
Take few minutes to reflect on what you've discovered through today's devotional.

Insights You Discovered To Reflect On

✐

✐

✐

Raising Your Ebenezer
An Ebenezer is an insight, a principle, or a life lesson that reminds us of what God has done - or is doing - for us on our journey through our tight places. What Ebenezer did you discover for yourself in today's devotional? Use this space to write it out here:

Notes

My Thoughts, Insights, And Reflections

_____

_____

_____

_____

_____

_____

_____

_____

_____

Day 31
Faith, Hope, and Love - The Broadest Place of All

"So now faith, hope, and love abide, these three;
but the greatest of these is love."
(1 Corinthians 13:13)

We began our devotional journey through the Psalms of tight places with "The Tightest Place of All" - fear. On this journey, we've seen how, in His dealings with us, God brings us out into "a broad place." As we bring our devotional journey to a conclusion, it's only right to review some of what we've discovered, and to conclude our journey with "the broadest place of all" - a place of faith, hope, and love.

Themes And Lessons

We've encountered a number of repeated themes on our shared journey through the Psalms of tight places. Of course, there's a reason behind the repetition of these themes. A repeated word becomes a theme, a repeated theme becomes a lesson, and repeated lessons become discipleship moments that challenge us to embrace life-transforming truths. In our spiritual brokenness, we learn with difficulty, forget easily, and often fail to apply lessons learned in one tight place to the challenge of the next tight place we encounter. Repetition is one of God's accommodations to our slow learning. It's His technique for building "synthetic learning," the ability to synthesize what we've learned in the context of one tight place, and to apply those lessons in the context of a new and different tight place. * Same God. Same lesson. Same truth. Just a new and different context. In the Kingdom of God, spiritual growth and maturity are the result of spiritual truth experienced over time, and frequently repeated for those of us who are slow learners. So, let's consider an abbreviated review of a handful of lessons we've encountered.

> In our spiritual brokenness, we learn with difficulty, forget easily, and often fail to apply lessons learned in one tight place to the challenge of the next tight place we encounter.

On our journey through tight places, we've discovered the importance of *remembering* God's past faithfulness in our lives to encourage us to trust Him in whatever we're currently going through. In the process we've witnessed the Psalmist's deep desire for *vindication*. His deep desire has caused us to recognize our own desire to see our walk of obedience and our trust in God's faithfulness vindicated, and to sense God's pleasure in the words "Well done, good and faithful servant." Along the way, we've learned that God doesn't want to see us put to shame, embarrassed, or publicly humiliated by what we're going through. No, His purpose is to teach us the importance of *obedience, humility* and *trust*. On more than one occasion, we've discovered how *fear* is both the most challenging and the most common tight place experienced by God's people, and how God wants to raise up a people who are spiritually *fearless* in their faith and obedience. And our journey has taught us that He is our *shepherd*, our *fortress*, and our *refuge* where we can dwell and seek shelter in *the Shadow of the Almighty*.

Having reflected on these Psalms and lessons, perhaps you've made a mental list of themes and lessons that have impacted you. What's on your list of lessons learned? Each person's list will be different, yet similar, because the same God who speaks truth into all of our lives also treats each of us as unique individuals. His love, concern, protection, and deliverance are personal. And so are His lessons.

A Greater Theme

But beyond our abbreviated list of themes and lessons, a *greater theme* emerges from the Psalms and from our journey through tight places. As we have noted before, lessons begun in the Old Testament frequently find their full development and fulfillment in the New Testament. And our *greater theme* is one of those lessons.

Somewhere around the year A.D. 55, a group of struggling Jesus-followers in the Greek city of Corinth wrestled with their own "tight place." Personal conflicts, spiritual immaturity, family issues, moral issues, and more, were forcing them into a collective tight place that threatened to tear their fellowship apart from the inside out. Into the *chaos* of that tight place, the Apostle Paul spoke some of the most impactful thoughts to be found in the New Testament. He spoke of the importance of faith, hope, and love in coming to a meaningful resolution of their tight place. He challenged them to examine their hearts, and to allow their struggle to produce greater spiritual depth and understanding regarding how God works among His people. Paul summed up his thoughts in a single, powerful statement, "So now faith, hope, and love abide, these three; but the greatest of these is love" (1 Corinthians 13:13). I'm pretty certain that David and the Psalmists would agree.

> In the Kingdom of God, faith, hope, and love are the ultimate broad place God desires for every believer.

Our *greater theme* from our journey through the Psalms is found in the three words used by Paul - faith, hope, and love. All three truths appear in the Psalms, and find their fully developed expression in the words of Paul to the Corinthians.

Day 31 - Faith, Hope, and Love - The Broadest Place of All

The word "trust" (*batach*, an Old Testament word for "faith") occurs 46 times in the Pslams. The word "hope" (*yachal*) occurs 19 times. And the word for "steadfast love" (*chesed*) occurs 123 times. In the context of the Psalms, *faith* is confidence in God and His dealings with us. *Hope* is faith waiting with patience for what God has promised. And *steadfast love* is God's covenant-keeping faithfulness to never abandon us, regardless of whatever tight place He finds us in. It is no exaggeration to say that the Psalmists understood the importance of "faith, hope, and love" in God's dealings with His people and their tight places. Paul simply completes what David and the Psalmists began. In the Kingdom of God, faith, hope, and love are the ultimate *broad place* God desires for every believer. A *faith* that conquers fear and doubt. A *hope* that expresses a faith willing to wait with patience for what God has promised. And a *love* for others that mirrors His steadfast covenant-keeping love for us.

In the Kingdom of God, the tight places of life and the lessons they teach us are God's fertile ground for our spiritual growth. There we re-discover the God of our salvation Who seeks us, finds us, meets us, protects us, makes room for us, teaches us, refines us, delivers us, and brings us out into a broad place of mature discipleship in His Kingdom. Every tight place He allows into our life is a stepping stone on our spiritual journey into the Kingdom of God. And each stepping stone becomes an *ebenezer* - a memorial stone - that empowers us to declare with the hymn writer,

> Every tight place He allows into our life is a stepping stone on our spiritual journey into the Kingdom of God.

"Here I raise my Ebenezer;
hither by thy help I'm come;
and I hope, by thy good pleasure,
safely to arrive at home." *

O Lord, our God, we worship You this day as the God of our journey through the tight places of life. You, O Lord, are a God merciful and gracious, slow to anger and abounding in steadfast love and faithfulness. You are our shepherd and our rock. You invite us to take refuge in the shelter of Your wings. Today, O Lord, let us abide with You in the shadow of the Almighty. Today we rejoice and give thanks that, in Your steadfast love, You never give up on us, regardless of where You find us. You are the One who refines us and tests us and leads us out of our tight place into a broad place of faith, hope, and love. Today we raise our ebenezer, our memorial stone of Your faithfulness and Your promise to bring us safely home to Your Kingdom. In all these things we rejoice and give thanks in the Name of Jesus Your Son, our Savior, and King. Amen.

Reflections On "Day 31 - Faith, Hope, & Love - The Broadest Place of All"
Take few minutes to reflect on what you've discovered through today's devotional.

Insights You Discovered To Reflect On

✍

✍

✍

Raising Your Ebenezer
An Ebenezer is an insight, a principle, or a life lesson that reminds us of what God has done - or is doing - for us on our journey through our tight places. What Ebenezer did you discover for yourself in today's devotional? Use this space to write it out here:

Notes

My Thoughts, Insights, And Reflections

_____

_____

_____

_____

_____

_____

_____

_____

Notes on the Psalms

Notes on An Introduction to Tight Places
* All of our documentary work is available for viewing on our documentary YouTube Channel: https://www.youtube.com/@MyRoadLeadsHome
* *tsarar* - root meaning, "to bind, be narrow, be in distress." See Harris, Archer, and Waltke, *Theological Wordbook of the Old Testament*, p 778, entry 1973 (hereafter, TWOT). While many Bible students rely on the Strong's numbering system for their word studies, TWOT is a standard and readily available reference work and is much more thorough. TWOT provides a Strong's number reference to the appropriate *Wordbook* entry.
* Leon Morris, *The Gospel According To John* (Grand Rapids: William B. Eerdmans Publishing Company, 1971), 7.
* The ESV Study Bible is available on Amazon at https://www.amazon.com/gp/aw/d/1433502410/

Notes on Day 1 - The Tightest Place of All
* A.W. Tozer, "Our Fruit Will Be What We Are" in *The Root of the Righteous* (Camp Hill: WingSpread Publishers, 1955, 1986), 2006 Edition, 119.
* In John 18:36, Jesus tells Pilate, the Roman Governor, that His Kingdom is not of this present world order (*cosmos*). The Kingdom of God represents a different *cosmos-order* from the present *cosmos-order* of this world, including the political order represented by Pilate and Rome. As Christians, our danger and our challenge comes when we confuse *Kingdom-cosmos* with the current *world cosmos-order*. We serve a different King, and we serve a different *Kingdom-cosmos*

Notes on Day 2, Psalm 3, Overwhelmed by a Thousand Troubles
* *rabab* - root meaning, "to become many, much." See TWOT, p 826, entry 2099.

Notes on Day 3, Psalm 4, Quietly Trusting
* *rachab* - root meaning, "to be wide." Note: "a colloquial expression practically defying translation." Also, "The term is one which has no single English equivalent." See TWOT, p 840, entry 2143.
* *thlipsis* - root meaning, "pressure, trouble, tribulation; great and pressing affliction." The Greek word occurs 45 times in the New Testament.
* In this context, cosmos refers to "the created order as it currently exists."
* *palah* - root meaning, "to be distinct, marked out." See TWOT, p 724, entry 1772.

Notes on Day 4, Psalm 6, Mercy and Grace
* *me'od* - root meaning, "exceedingly, much, force, abundance" hence "vehemently." See TWOT, p 487, entry 1134.
* *chanan* - root meaning, "to be gracious, to pity." It is also described as "an action from a superior to an inferior who has no real claim for gracious treatment." And again, "it often has the sense of showing kindness to the poor and needy." See TWOT, p 302, entry 694.

Notes on Day 5, Psalm 7, Accusations and Innocence - Part 1
* *chasah* - root meaning, "to seek refuge, to flee for protection," fig. "to put trust in, confide, hope in." See TWOT, p 307, entry 700.
* *'ayab* - root meaning, "to be an enemy" also "enmity, hatred." See TWOT, p 36, entry 78.

Notes on Day 7, Psalm 9, A Stronghold of the Poor
* *sapar* - root meanng, "to count, to recount" by extension, "to declare, to show forth." See TWOT, p 632, entry 1540.

* *shapat* (verb) and *mishpat* (noun) are from the same root family, root meaning "to judge, to govern" by extension, "to vindicate." TWOT, p 947, entry 2443.

* A.W. Tozer, "Faith Dares To Fail" in *Born After Midnight* (Camp Hill: WingSpread Publishers, 1959, 1987), 2008 Edition, 69.

* *misgab* - (from sagab) - root meaning, "to be inaccessibly high" hence, "high place, refuge." See TWOT, p 871, entry 2234a.

* *dak* - root meaning, "crushed, oppressed," See TWOT, p 189, entry 429a.

* *'ani* - (from *'ana*) - root meaning, "Poor, weak, afflicted, humble" and "primarily a person suffering some kind of disability." See TWOT, p 682, entry 1652d.

* *'ebyon* - (from *'aba*) - root meaning, "One in a state of wanting, a needy or poor person." See TWOT, p 4, entry 3a.

* *'anaw* - root meaning, "humble, meek," the intended outcome of affliction, "humility." See TWOT, p 682, entry 1652a.

Notes on Day 8, Psalm 13, How Long, O Lord?
* Dr. King distilled his observation from an 1853 sermon by the Reverend Theodore Parker who said, "I don't pretend to understand the moral universe. The arc is a long one. My eye reaches but little ways. I cannot calculate the curve and complete the figure by experience of sight. I can divine it by conscience. And from what I see I am sure it bends toward justice."

Notes on Day 9, Psalm 20, The "Golden Rule"
* The phrase "day of trouble" occurs in Psalm 20:1; 27:5; 41:1; 50:15. It also occurs in 5 other places in the Old Testament.

Notes on Day 10, Psalm 23, Our Shepherd In Tight Places
* Psalm 117 is the shortest of all the Psalms, if you're wondering.
* *tsalmawet* - (from *tsalal*), root meaning, "to be or grow dark, deep darkness." See TWOT, p 7676, entry 1921b.

Notes on Day 11, Psalm 25, Redeemed Out of All Our Tight Places
* *'ayab* - root meaning, "to be an enemy" also "enmity, hatred." See TWOT, p 36, entry 78.
* *racham* - root meaning, to love deeply, have mercy, be compassionate." See TWOT, p 841, entry 2146a.
* *chesed* - root meaning, "lovingkindness, steadfast love, mercy." See TWOT, p 305, entry 698a. *chesed* occurs 247 times in the Old Testament, and half of those (127) are in the Psalms.
* *sod* - root meaning, "counsel," emphasis on confidentiality, hence, friendship. See TWOT, p 619, entry 1471a.

Notes on Day 12, Psalm 27, "One Thing"
* A.W. Tozer, *The Knowledge of the Holy* (New York: Harper & Row, 1961), 9.
* ra'a - root meaning, "bed, evil." See TWOT, p 854, entry 2191.
* A.W. Tozer, "Faith Brings Committal" in *The Root of the Righteous* (Camp Hill: WingSpread Publishers, 1955, 1986), 2006 Edition, 52.

Notes on Day 13, Psalm 31, From A Tight Place to a Broad Place
* *bosh* - root meaning, "to be ashamed, to fall into disgrace." See TWOT, p 97, entry 222.
* *hebel* - root meaning, "vapor, breath, vanity." See TWOT, p 204, entry 463a.
* The words "distress" (verse 9) and "adversaries" (verse 11) are both derived from our Hebrew root word for "tight places."

Notes on Day 14, Psalm 32, A Tight Place Called Sin
* *pesha'* - root meaning, "rebellion, revolt, transgression." See TWOT, p 740, entry 1846a.
* *chata'a* - root meaning, "to miss the way," then "sin." See TWOT, p 277, entry 638d.
* *'awon* - (from *'awa* meaning "to bend, twist, or distort"), root meaning, "iniquity, guilt, punishment for guilt." See TWOT, p 650, entry 1577a.
* *sether* - (from *sathar*, "to hide or conceal"), root meaning, "hiding place." See TWOT, p 636, entry 1551a.

Notes on Day 15, Psalm 34, Celebrating Deliverance
* Scholars generally agree that the name "Abimelech" used in Psalm 34 is probably an alternative name of King Achish in 1 Samuel 21.
* *'anaw* - root meaning, "humble, meek," the intended outcome of affliction, "humility." See TWOT, p 682, entry 1652a.
* *magor* - root meaning, "fear, terror" and "the terror of human caprice" [sudden or impulsive idea or action]. See TWOT, p 156, entry 332a.

Notes on Day 16, Psalm 37, Trusting and Waiting
* *chara* - root meaning, "to burn, to be kindled." See TWOT, p. 322, entry 736.
* *'olam* - root meaning, "forever, everlasting, perpetual," primarily a description of "indefinite continuance" whether past or future. See TWOT, p 672-673, entry 1631. The Greek Septuagint translation of the Old Testament generally translates *'olam* with the Greek *aion* or "age."

Notes on Day 17, Psalms 42-43, Spiritual Thirst in Tight Places.
* While Psalms 42 and 43 can be read and viewed separately, scholars frequently treat them as "two parts of a single, close-knit poem," which is what we are doing here. See Derek Kidner, *Psalms 1-72: An Introduction and Commentary* (Downers Grove: IVP Academic, 1973) 182.
* *"The Dark Night of the Soul."* Originally a reference to a poem of St. John of the Cross (1542 - 1591), more recently it has become a popular phrase to describe a crisis of faith, or a difficult and painful period in someone's life.

Notes on Day 18, Psalm 44, The Greater Struggle
* This is Derek Kidner's observation, too. "Momentarily it sees that God's people are caught up in a war that is more than local: the struggle of 'the kings of the earth . . . against the Lord and his Anointed' (2:2)." See Derek Kidner, *Psalms 1-72: An Introduction and Commentary* (Downers Grove: IVP Academic, 1973) 186.
* Daniel was given insight into this spiritual reality in Daniel Chapter 10. See also Ephesians 6:10-20, I Peter 5:8-9, and Jude.
* See Day 14, "A Tight Place Called Sin" for more about tight places caused by personal sin.

Notes on Day 19, Psalm 46, God, Our Fortress
* My thanks to Blanca Ayre, a devotional writer from Hays, Kansas, for sharing this insight.

Notes on Day 21, Psalm 69, Exhausted And Overwhelmed - Part 1
* *cherpa* (from *charap*) - root meaning "to reproach, blaspheme, defy" hence "reproach." TWOT, p 325, entry 749a.

Notes on Day 23, Psalm 71, From Youth To Old Age.
* A.W. Tozer, "True Faith Brings Committal," in *The Root Of The Righteous* (WingSpread Publishers: Camp Hill, PA, 1986), 51.
* *mopet* - root meaning, "wonder, miracle, sign, portent." TWOT, p 66, entry 52a.

Notes on Day 24, Psalm 74, When Everything Crashes And Burns
* *'oth*, (from *'awa*) - root meaning, "sign, mark, token, ensign, standard, miraculous sign." TWOT, p 18, entry 41a.

Notes on Day 25, Psalm 77, A Deeper Day of Trouble.
* Concerning the "dark night of the soul," see above **Notes on Day 17, Psalms 42-43.**

Notes on Day 26, Psalm 81, A Tight Place Called Meribah
* *bachan* - root meaning, "to exam, to try, to test." TWOT, p100, entry 230. The 9 occurrences of *bachan* in the Psalms are 7:9; 11:4& 5; 17:3; 26:2; 66:10; 81:7; 95:9; 139:23

Notes on Day 27, Psalm 86, Regaining Our Focus
* In addition to today's Psalm, the phrase "poor and needy" appears in Day 7, Psalm 9; Day 16, Psalm 37; Day 24: Psalm 74.
* On God's concern for the poor and needy see also 1 Samuel 2:8; Job 5:15-16.
* *chasid* - root meaning, "holy one, saint." TWOT, p 307, entry 698.
* See definitions in Day 7 above.
* *rabab* - root meaning, "to become many, much." TWOT, 826, entry 2088. This Hebrew root is used elsewhere in Scripture to describe "multitude" or "ten thousand." The eight occurrences of God's "abounding" or "great" steadfast love are: Exodus 34:6; Numbers 14:18; Nehemiah 9:17; Psalm 86:5, 15; Psalm 103:8; Joel 2:13; Jonah 4:2.

Notes on Day 28, Psalm 91, In The Shadow of The Almighty
* John Piper, "Slain In The Shadow Of The Almighty,"
https://www.desiringgod.org/articles/slain-in-the-shadow-of-the-almighty

Notes on Day 29, Psalm 102, When God Hides Himself
* *'ani* - (from *'ana*) - root meaning, "Poor, weak, afflicted, humble" and "primarily a person suffering some kind of disability." See TWOT, p 682, entry 1652d.
* *'ataph* - root meaning, "to be feeble, faint, grow weak," a general sense of being physically exhausted and overwhelmed. TWOT, p 661, entry 1607.
* *sinach* - root meaning, a "meditation" or "complaint." TWOT, p 875, entry 2255a.
* This is a more complete list of passages that talk about God hiding face: Job 13:24; Psalm 13:1; 27:9; 44:24; 51:9; 69:17; 88:14; 102:2; 104:29; 143:7; 22:24.
* *transience* - the state, fact, or condition of lasting only for a short time, such as "the transience of life and happiness."

Notes on Day 30, Psalm 107, Thanksgiving for Steadfast Love
* *chesed* - root meaning, "lovingkindness, steadfast love, mercy." See TWOT, p 305, entry 698a. *chesed* occurs 247 times in the Old Testament, and half of those (127) are in the Psalms.
* *'aheb* - root meaning, "to love, like, be in love, lovely." The Hebrew word describing an emotional attraction or attachment, including love between people, or the love of things by people.
* I tell the story of that camp in my book, *A Place To Exist: The True and Untold Story of Camp Hope and Homelessness in Spokane* (Spokane: Rising River Media, 2023). Available on Amazon at https://www.amazon.com/Place-Exist-Untold-Homlessness-Spokane/dp/b0cjddk8g6/

Notes on Day 31, Faith, Hope, and Love - The Broadest Place of All
* By "Synthetic learning" (or "Synthesizing," also called "information synthesis" in educational circles) we mean the process of taking biblical truths, principles, and lessons learned in one or more contexts ("tight places") and applying them to a new and different context so we can

understanding how they contribute to our discipleship in the Kingdom of God. For an application in educational research and writing, see
https://www.uis.edu/learning-hub/writing-resources/handouts/learning-hub/synthesizing-research
* From the hymn, "Come Thou Fount of Every Blessing" (Lyrics by Robert Robinson [1735-1790]; Music by John Wyeth [1770-1858]. Ebenezer is a compound Hebrew word meaning literally "stone of the help"; a memorial stone erected by the prophet Samuel to mark the place, just north of Jerusalem, where God helped Israel defeat the Philistines. See 1 Samuel 7:12.

Appendix
All the Psalms of Tight Places

Psalm	Passage
Psalm 3:1-2	O LORD, how many are my *foes*! Many are rising against me; many are saying of my soul, "There is no salvation for him in God."
Psalm 4:1	Answer me when I call, O God of my righteousness! You have **given me relief** when I was in **distress**. Be gracious to me and hear my prayer!
Psalm 6:7	My eye wastes away because of grief; it grows weak because of all my **foes**.
Psalm 7:4, 6	if I have repaid my friend with evil or plundered my **enemy** without cause . . . Arise, O LORD, in your anger; lift yourself up against the fury of my **enemies**; awake for me; you have appointed a judgment.
Psalm 8:2	Out of the mouth of babies and infants, you have established strength because of your **foes**, to still the enemy and the avenger.
Psalm 9:9	The LORD is a stronghold for the oppressed, a stronghold in times of **trouble**.
Psalm 10:1, 5	Why, O LORD, do you stand far away? Why do you hide yourself in times of **trouble**? His ways prosper at all times; your judgments are on high, out of his sight; as for all his **foes**, he puffs at them.
Psalm 13:3-4	Consider and answer me, O LORD my God; light up my eyes, lest I sleep the sleep of death, lest my enemy say, "I have prevailed over him," lest my **foes** rejoice because I am shaken.
Psalm 18:6	In my **distress** I called upon the LORD; to my God I cried for help. From his temple he heard my voice, and my cry to him reached his ears.
Psalm 20:1	May the LORD answer you in the day of **trouble**! May the name of the God of Jacob protect you!
Psalm 22:10-11	On you was I cast from my birth, and from my mother's womb you have been my God. Be not far from me, for **trouble** is near, and there is none to help.
Psalm 23:5	You prepare a table before me in the presence of my **enemies**; you anoint my head with oil; my cup overflows.

Psalm 25:16-18, 22	Turn to me and be gracious to me, for I am lonely and afflicted. The *troubles* of my heart are enlarged; bring me out of my distresses. Consider my affliction and my trouble, and forgive all my sins . . . . Redeem Israel, O God, out of all his *troubles*.
Psalm 27:2, 12	When evildoers assail me to eat up my flesh, my *adversaries* and foes, it is they who stumble and fall. Give me not up to the will of my *adversaries*; for false witnesses have risen against me, and they breathe out violence.
Psalm 31:7-9, 11	I will rejoice and be glad in your steadfast love, because you have seen my affliction; you have known the *distress* of my soul, and you have not delivered me into the hand of the enemy; you have set my feet in a broad place. Be gracious to me, O LORD, for I am in *distress*; my eye is wasted from grief; my soul and my body also. Because of all my *adversaries* I have become a reproach, especially to my neighbors, and an object of dread to my acquaintances; those who see me in the street flee from me.
Psalm 32:7	You are a hiding place for me; you preserve me from *trouble*; you surround me with shouts of deliverance.
Psalm 34:6, 17	This poor man *cried*, and the LORD heard him and saved him out of all his *troubles*. When the righteous *cry* for help, the LORD hears and delivers them out of all their *troubles*.
Psalm 37:39	The salvation of the righteous is from the LORD; he is their *stronghold* in the time of *trouble*.
Psalm 42:10	As with a deadly wound in my bones, my *adversaries* taunt me, while they say to me all the day long, "Where is your God?"
Psalm 44:5-10	Through you we push down our *foes*; through your name we tread down those who rise up against us . . . But you have saved us from our *foes* and have put to shame those who hate us . . . You have made us turn back from the *foe*, and those who hate us have gotten spoil.
Psalm 46:1	God is our refuge and strength, a very present *help* in *trouble*.
Psalm 50:14-15	Offer to God a sacrifice of thanksgiving, and perform your vows to the Most High, and call upon me in the day of *trouble*; I will *deliver* you, and you shall *glorify* me."
Psalm 54:6-7	With a freewill offering I will sacrifice to you; I will give thanks to your name, O LORD, for it is good. For he has delivered me from every *trouble*, and my eye has looked in triumph on my enemies.
Psalm 59:16	But I will sing of your strength; I will sing aloud of your steadfast love in the morning. For you have been to me a fortress and a refuge in the *day of my distress*.

Psalm 60:10-12	Have you not rejected us, O God? You do not go forth, O God, with our armies. Oh, grant us help against the *foe*, for vain is the salvation of man! With God we shall do valiantly; it is he who will tread down our *foes*.
Psalm 66:13-14	I will come into your house with burnt offerings; I will perform my vows to you, that which my lips uttered and my mouth promised when I was in *trouble*.
Psalm 69:16-17, 19	Answer me, O LORD, for your steadfast love is good; according to your abundant mercy, turn to me. Hide not your face from your servant, for I am in *distress*; make haste to answer me. You know my reproach, and my shame and my dishonor; my *foes* are all known to you.
Psalm 71:19-20	Your righteousness, O God, reaches the high heavens. You who have done great things, O God, who is like you? You who have made me see *many troubles* and calamities will revive me again; from the depths of the earth you will bring me up again.
Psalm 74:4, 9-10, 23	Your **foes** have roared in the midst of your meeting place; they set up their own signs for signs. We do not see our signs; there is no longer any prophet, and there is none among us who knows how long. How long, O God, is the *foe* to scoff? Is the enemy to revile your name forever? Do not forget the clamor of your **foes**, the uproar of those who rise against you, which goes up continually!
Psalm 77:2	In *the day of my trouble* I seek the Lord; in the night my hand is stretched out without wearying; my soul refuses to be comforted.
Psalm 78:42-43, 49, 60-61, 66	They did not remember his power or the day when he redeemed them from the *foe*, when he performed his signs in Egypt and his marvels in the fields of Zoan . . . He let loose on them his burning anger, wrath, indignation, and *distress*, a company of destroying angels . . . He forsook his dwelling at Shiloh, the tent where he dwelt among mankind, and delivered his power to captivity, his glory to the hand of the *foe* . . . And he put his *adversaries* to rout; he put them to everlasting shame.
Psalm 81:7 & 14	In *distress* you called, and I delivered you; I answered you in the secret place of thunder; I tested you at the waters of Meribah. I would soon subdue their enemies and turn my hand against their *foes*.
Psalm 86:7	In *the day of my trouble* I call upon you, for you answer me.
Psalm 89:23 & 42	I will crush his *foes* before him and strike down those who hate him. You have exalted the right hand of his *foes*; you have made all his enemies rejoice.
Psalm 91:15	When he calls to me, I will answer him; I will be with him in *trouble*; I will rescue him and honor him.

Psalm 97:3	Fire goes before him and burns up his *adversaries* all around.
Psalm 102:2	Do not hide your face from me in the day of my *distress*! Incline your ear to me; answer me speedily in the day when I call!
Psalm 105:24	And the LORD made his people very fruitful and made them stronger than their *foes*.
Psalm 106:11 & 44	And the waters covered their *adversaries*; not one of them was left. Nevertheless, he looked upon their *distress*, when he heard their cry.
Psalm 107:2, 6, 13, 19, 28	2 - Let the redeemed of the LORD say so, whom he has redeemed from *trouble* 6 - Then they cried to the LORD in their *trouble*, and he delivered them from their distress. 13 - Then they cried to the LORD in their *trouble*, and he delivered them from their distress. 19 - Then they cried to the LORD in their *trouble*, and he delivered them from their distress. 28 - Then they cried to the LORD in their *trouble*, and he delivered them from their distress.
Psalm 108:12-13	Oh grant us help against the *foe*, for vain is the salvation of man! With God we shall do valiantly; it is he who will tread down our *foes*.
Psalm 112:6-8	For the righteous will never be moved; he will be remembered forever. He is not afraid of bad news; his heart is firm, trusting in the LORD. His heart is steady; he will not be afraid, until he looks in triumph on his *adversaries*.
Psalm 116:3	The snares of death encompassed me; the pangs of Sheol laid hold on me; I suffered *distress* and anguish.
Psalm 119:139, 143, 157	My zeal consumes me, because my *foes* forget your words. *Trouble* and anguish have found me out, but your commandments are my delight. Many are my persecutors and my *adversaries*, but I do not swerve from your testimonies.
Psalm 120:1	In my *distress* I called to the LORD, and he answered me.
Psalm 129:1-2	"Greatly have they *afflicted* me from my youth"— let Israel now say— "Greatly have they *afflicted* me from my youth, yet they have not prevailed against me.
Psalm 136:23-25	It is he who remembered us in our low estate, for his steadfast love endures forever; and rescued us from our *foes*, for his steadfast love endures forever; He who gives food to all flesh, for his steadfast love endures forever.

Psalm 138:7	Though I walk in the midst of *trouble*, you preserve my life; you stretch out your hand against the wrath of my enemies, and your right hand delivers me.
Psalm 142:1-2	With my voice I cry out to the LORD; with my voice I plead for mercy to the LORD. I pour out my complaint before him; I tell my *trouble* before him.
Psalm 143:11, 12	For your name's sake, O LORD, preserve my life! In your righteousness bring my soul out of *trouble*! And in your steadfast love you will cut off my enemies, and you will destroy all the *adversaries* of my soul, for I am your servant.

www.ingramcontent.com/pod-product-compliance
Lightning Source LLC
Chambersburg PA
CBHW061750120626
46550CB00005B/1944